STERLING EPICURE
New York

An Imprint of Sterling Publishing
387 Park Avenue South
New York, NY 10016

Cover and Interior design by HellaCrisis with Johnny Por Taing and Albert Ignacio
Food photography by Josh Shaub and David Belisle
Other photography by TONE and King Texas
Video stills from Kalim Armstrong and Terence Teh
Food illustrations by HellaCrisis
All other illustrations by HellaCrisis with Nathaniel Matthews,
Whitney Young, Kevin Harris, Daniel Choe and John Toga Cox

ISBN 978-1-4027-9429-2

Distributed in Canada by Sterling Publishing
c/o Canadian Manda Group, 165 Dufferin Street
Toronto, Ontario, Canada M6K 3H6
Distributed in the United Kingdom by GMC Distribution Services
Castle Place, 166 High Street, Lewes, East Sussex, England BN7 1XU
Distributed in Australia by Capricorn Link (Australia) Pty. Ltd.
P.O. Box 704, Windsor, NSW 2756, Australia

For information about custom editions, special sales, and premium and corporate purchases, please contact Sterling Special Sales at 800-805-5489 or specialsales@sterlingpublishing.com.

Manufactured in China

2 4 6 8 10 9 7 5 3 1

www.sterlingpublishing.com

THE **DANTE FRIED CHICKEN** EXPERIENCE

RIDE OR FRY

BY **DANTE GONZALES** AND **THE DFC CREW**
WITH **TERENCE TEH**

STERLING EPICURE

New York

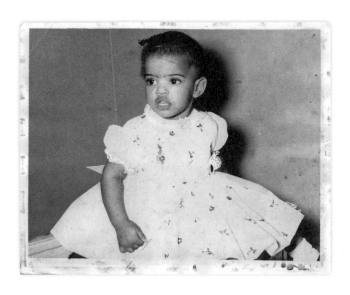

In memory of my mommy,
Kim Lorraine Forrest

CONTENTS

CHAPTER 3: HYPE MAN
CLASSIC SIDES, SALADS & VEGGIES

PG **108**

CHAPTER 6: DFC BASICS— SPICES, STOCKS & SAUCES

DFC SHOW "SCOTTIE B'S BIRTHDAY PARTY" EPISODE

SCOTTIE B RYE RYE MACHINEDRUM JIMM...
...ASWIFT PURSUIT GROOVES THEOPHILUS...
...HLOE ZAD DA BEAST KISSEY ASPLUN...
...KODKUIT DJ SAY WUT TRYFE KENNEDY DJ...
...B...CHMONKEY JESSE BOYKINS III

...PUMPKIN PIE FRY CHICKEN TOFU COCONU...
...CASSEROLE TOMATILLO COLLARD GREENS...
...BLACK EYE PEAS

...PRIL 6TH | 5PM | GALOPAGOS | 70 N 6TH ST BROOKLYN

THE DFC VIBE

THE ATTITUDE BEHIND CELEBRATION FOOD!

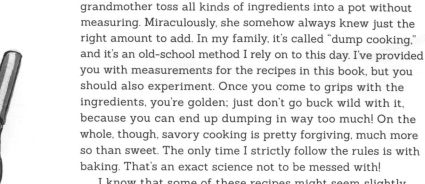

I remember hanging out in the kitchen watching my grandmother toss all kinds of ingredients into a pot without measuring. Miraculously, she somehow always knew just the right amount to add. In my family, it's called "dump cooking," and it's an old-school method I rely on to this day. I've provided you with measurements for the recipes in this book, but you should also experiment. Once you come to grips with the ingredients, you're golden; just don't go buck wild with it, because you can end up dumping in way too much! On the whole, though, savory cooking is pretty forgiving, much more so than sweet. The only time I strictly follow the rules is with baking. That's an exact science not to be messed with!

I know that some of these recipes might seem slightly intimidating, like, "Whoa, that ingredient list looks crazy!" But don't get overwhelmed on me, it's all about how you prepare. When I cook, I like to have all of my ingredients and items (except the refrigerated ones) in front of me and pre-prepped. This makes for a way easier and quicker process; and in this distracting world we live in, pre-prep helps you avoid missing steps.

You'll also notice that I didn't break down how long each step takes (prep, cook, clean-up times, etc.). This is because I can't account for every aspect of your life: how late you roll in to your crib; whether you have to cook your kids' food first; or you only have one hand . . . the reality is that in this world today, we never have enough time.

My food is old-school, and the cuisine is what I call Transatlantic African. It's a mix of the three basic culinary traditions that make up the African diaspora: the cuisines of Africa, Europe, and indigenous America, from Peru to the Dominican Republic, New Orleans to Cape Cod. Take gumbo, for instance: it's a perfect example of Transatlantic Africanism. You have this big pot of simmering cultures where every ingredient in the basic recipe has its own heritage. The okra is essential, representing the African ancestry that forms gumbo's foundation and gives this heirloom dish its name (*gumbo* is another word for okra in some parts of Africa). The European influence in gumbo can be traced through the Italian herbs and, of course, the rich, smoky, Andouille sausage, a German delicacy with a French name. Finally, Native American filé powder (ground sassafras leaves), an indigenous American element, completes the culinary

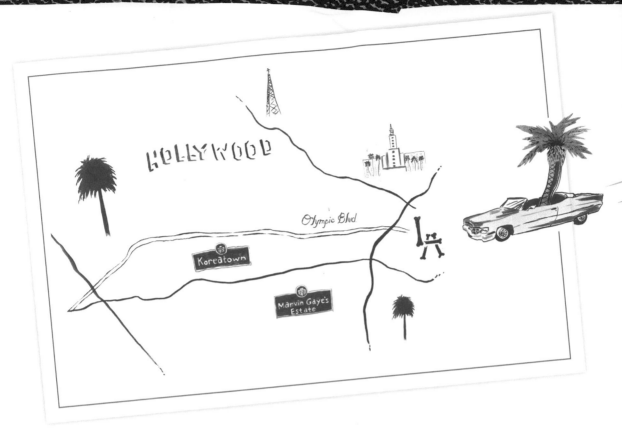

melting pot. And it's not just agriculture and spices that are represented in gumbo—there's also the roux, made from a classic French technique. Gumbo wouldn't be gumbo without this potent collision of cultures, the exchange of ingredients, and converging cooking methods.

With Transatlantic African Cuisine, I'm simply following my heritage and interpreting the connection among Asia, Africa, Europe, and America in a modern way. It's a celebration of all the different traditions that have developed and the trading that's occurred throughout the history of food.

My food is also heavily influenced by my family's Creole cuisine. Already under the sway of multiple influences (Caribbean, African, Native American, and European), Creole cooks are always looking to be inspired by other cultures. Creole food is the most eccentric of the South, and that's how many would describe my cooking: eccentric. I like to mix unexpected flavors and textures and see what comes out of it. I also draw inspiration from the Mexican and Asian cultures and influences that were part of my environment growing up in Southern California.

I continue to mix flavors and customs: I've had the opportunity to cook up across the UK and Europe and love exchanging culinary concepts with the people I meet there. When I first got on the plane to Europe I had no idea what to expect, but I soon discovered that Europeans have many long-held family traditions just like we do—I could taste the love in the food. It would be awesome to fry chicken in even more exotic locations, like Tokyo or Moscow, and bring back something new.

An explanation of my culinary philosophy wouldn't be complete without mention of a state of mind I maintain in my cooking: Eco-fresh, yo! My grandmother was way ahead of her time regarding slow food, sustainability, and locally sourced ingredients, and all of that is extra important to me now. Back in the day, being eco-conscious wasn't even recognized yet, but Grans was already doing it. Eco-fresh, yo! is about being earth-conscious and respecting a balance in nature that has been in existence since time began. And it's not as hard as it sounds: being earth-conscious can be as simple as making our own tomato sauce from scratch with locally grown tomatoes. It's a balancing act of give and take, create and waste, and making sure our practices and resources coexist harmoniously. Don't forget, small changes can help us out a million times over. Eco-fresh, yo! Let's go!

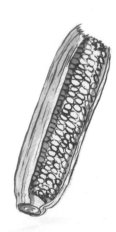

As you embark on new cooking adventures, I hope you are inspired by this book to push your own culinary boundaries. Food can take you around the world or it can take you right back home. Or—this is the best one—it can do both at the same time. Have fun.

DON'T SWEAT THE TECHNIQUE

First off, I want to emphasize that this book isn't about making 30-minute meals that are meant to be consumed in five. It's not about convenience food. Everything here is food you make when you've got the time to really cook and enjoy what you're eating. A lot of what I've included here is inspired by my family, and they didn't eat these dishes on the daily. Most of my family was dirt-rock poor! These recipes are about special occasions and celebrations—even now, I don't eat crazy fried chicken every day! This is the kind of food I would cook with my grandmother every Sunday, on Martin Luther King Day, the Fourth of July, or even Cinco de Mayo. Food that, above all, tastes damn good and is honest about its ingredients. I'm not into being an elitist chef. For me it's more important to celebrate life among people drawn together by folklore, fire, and fried chicken than to cultivate esoteric ingredients.

Aside from celebrating with food, my cooking is also about connecting to our elders' ways. My methods are old-school updated with a modern sensibility—what I call Slow Skool cooking. Slow Skool is the antidote to industrialized cooking—the Kryptonite! I don't expect home cooks to make everything from scratch every day of their lives, of course, but I like to encourage people to honor their heritage and to acquire actual know-how. There's nothing wrong with cooking for convenience, but there's with a lot to be learned from "back-in-the-day" techniques and the DIY philosophy—let's bring them back.

As you make your way through *Ride or Fry*, know that it's important to *characterize* your food. In other words, give your food its own character or personality. Take spicing, for example. I've kept everything to a medium spice level, but you should feel free to experiment. Look at the spicing in my recipes as a guideline only. You've got to bond with different ingredients in your own personal way. If you don't like celery seed, you can omit it. If white pepper's not your thing, leave it out. It's going to taste different, but you'll be giving your version of this food its own character. I personally love celery seed and white pepper in my Credit Crunch Fried Chicken (page 30), so I go a little heavy-handed on those spices in the Fried Chicken Spice Mix (page 190); that's how I make it distinct. Now it's up to you to make your food unique, too.

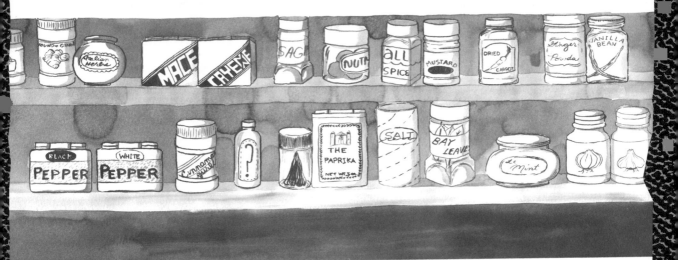

⟨DFC⟩ PANTRY

We about to get pantry wit' it and get you set up with a certified DFC-laced kitchen. I'm going to show you two options for your spice, herb, and basic condiments game. The first is all about the essentials—it's the DFC Bare Bones set-up—so that you're good to go. Then there's the DFC Swagger Pantry for the more eccentric, advanced cook. There are also kitchen-tool recommendations to help it all go smoothly.

When people eat my food, they always say the seasoning just pops right out at you—it's one of my major signature moves. A lot of that comes down to the control you have with home-blended herbs and spices vs. supermarket pre-made mixes. Don't get me wrong, I have nothing against the likes of Lawry's Seasoned Salt or Old Bay. They're all-time classics and I do use them, but I never rely on them exclusively and you shouldn't either. I always doctor up the flavors by adding new spices to the mix; I got to add that DFC character into the cooking.

For me, the crux of dry spicing ingredients is simple. Alongside salt, the cornerstones are black pepper, granulated garlic, granulated onion, and paprika. I like hot and sweet paprika but there's also smoked, Spanish, and Hungarian paprika, too. These base spices are not only at the heart of my cooking, but old-school cooking worldwide.

In terms of herbs, try out both fresh and dry varieties to see which you prefer in different dishes; keep in mind that there's a spectrum of flavors spanning dry and fresh. For instance, dried fennel seed is super potent, with a strong medicinal flavor whereas fresh fennel is mild and juicy with light, celery-like, aniseed undertones. On the flip, fresh basil makes dishes pop much more than a sprinkling of dry basil, but you can't cook the fresh for too long or the heat will kill the flavor. Whatever the case, it's important to crush your herbs and spices before adding them to the dish; this releases the aromatics and natural oils. You can do it with a spice grinder or with a pestle and mortar. Use whichever method feels right—to *you*.

THE BARE-BONES DFC PANTRY

When buying spices, it's often possible to buy in bulk, which can save you a lot of money. Hold off buying in quantity, though, until you know which spices you like and use the most. Stocking a pantry can take a while, so it's a good idea to think about buying one or two of these items each time you go to the grocery store instead of all at once.

SPICES

- Ground paprika (Hungarian or Spanish)
- Granulated garlic
- Granulated onion
- Cayenne pepper or crushed pepper flakes
- Five-peppercorn blend
- Celery seed or leaf
- Bay leaves
- Chinese Five Spice powder
- Dried premixed herbs (such as herbes de Provence and dried mixed Italian herbs)
- American chili powder
- Curry powder
- Cumin seeds or powder
- Dried sage
- Dried cinnamon
- Dried nutmeg powder
- Dried ginger powder
- Dried allspice powder
- Dried turmeric
- Brown sugar
- White sesame seeds
- Black sesame seeds
- Poppy seeds
- Raw or roasted nuts (cashews, peanuts, almonds, and pecans)

- Dried cranberries
- Raisins
- Brown sugar
- Real vanilla extract
- Almond extract or paste
- Molasses
- Raw honey
- Bragg's liquid amino acids
- Bragg's apple cider vinegar
- Extra virgin olive oil
- Vegetable oil with a high smoke point (such as canola, peanut, or safflower)
- Coconut water
- Miso paste
- Peanut butter

SWAGGER ADD-ONS

- Dried sweet paprika granules or chopped
- Dried chopped chives
- Dried chopped onion
- Dried chopped garlic
- Dried leeks
- Dried seaweed
- White peppercorn
- Pink peppercorn
- 3 varieties of dried Mexican chilies (such as poblano, aji panco, and chipotle)
- Multiple varieties of chopped dried herbs (like thyme, marjoram, basil, and rosemary)
- Freeze dried carrots
- Preserved lemons
- Saffron strands
- Dutch-process cocoa powder
- Dried lavender
- Coriander powder
- Vanilla bean pod
- Rye seeds
- Whole nutmeg

- Cardamom pods
- Whole cinnamon sticks
- Ground mace
- Dried honey granules
- Dried apricots
- Dried cherries
- Dates
- Cashews
- Peanuts
- Agave or rice nectar
- Real maple syrup

COOKING SPIRITS

- White and red wine
- Jameson whiskey
- Ketel One vodka
- Zaya rum
- Chocolate wine
- Boddingtons Pub Ale
- Guinness stout

BASIC TOOLS

- 6-in. sauté pan
- 10-in. cast-iron skillet or frying pan
- 12-in. cast-iron skillet or frying pan
- 5- to 6-quart Dutch oven
- 8-quart stock pot
- 8-in. chef's knife
- 3- to 4-in. paring knife
- 9 x 13-in. glass baking dish
- 9-in. pie plate
- 2 baking sheets
- 2 to 3 baking racks (they come in sets as well)
- Meat thermometer
- Candy thermometer (used as a deep-fryer thermometer too)
- Oven thermometer
- Cuisinart spice and nut grinder
- Blender

SWAGGER EQUIPMENT

- 3-quart sauce pot
- 30-quart stock pot
- 13-in. wok
- Large ceramic or glazed cast-iron casserole or baking dish
- Cuisinart hand mixer
- Kitchen-Aid food processor
- Kitchen-Aid stand mixer
- Waring deep fat fryer
- Cheesecloth
- Fine mesh sieve
- Cut-resistant glove

KEY INGREDIENTS FOR VEGAN DISHES

- Earth Balance Natural Buttery Spread
- Earth Balance Shortening
- Earth Balance Coconut Spread
- Follow Your Heart Vegenaise
- Follow Your Heart sour cream
- Follow Your Heart cream cheese
- Quorn veggie naked cutlets
- RiceMellow

DFC OILS

Peanut Oil: With tons of omega fats and amino acids, peanut oil is super healthy and has a high smoke point that makes it perfect for frying. I like both the unfiltered and the lighter, refined versions that you can get from Asian stores worldwide.

Olive Oil: This classic oil is fruity, healthy, versatile, and good for general-purpose usage. While you can't deep fry in olive oil, it's still a cupboard essential.

Canola Oil: A cheaper alternative to peanut oil, canola oil also has a high smoke point, making it another great go-to for frying.

Seasoning Oils: In the same way that you can flavor water with herbs and veggies to make stock, you can add flavor to oils before frying up. To do it, drop some dried onion, garlic, and celery, or woody herbs such as rosemary and bay leaves into your cooking oil of choice. For extra flavor, add ham hocks or turkey necks to the oil while it's warming up (remove them before frying). Notice that when the oil is hot enough to fry, the veggies and herbs will be nicely browned and ready for the chicken.

←KITCHEN→ SAFETY TIPS

~ FRY SAFELY ▾

There's a lot of frying going on in this book, so let's go over how to cook safely with boiling oil.

The first thing to keep in mind when frying is never, ever get a glass of water or any other liquid that is not cooking oil where it can spill into the fryer. If it does, it will vaporize instantly and can violently spray hot oil in all directions. It is for this reason you should never try to put out a grease fire with water.

Most kitchen fires happen because someone started heating fat or oil and forgot about it or bumped into the vessel containing the hot oil, spilling it onto an open flame. Grease fires are very hard to extinguish but they must be quickly brought under control. But let me repeat: DO NOT ATTEMPT TO PUT A GREASE FIRE OUT WITH WATER! The best way to contain a grease fire is to use a fire extinguisher, but if you don't have one (you definitely should!), use flour. Liberally cover the fire in flour to smother the flames.

DEEP-FAT FRYERS

FYI, I like to do a lot of my small-scale frying in a large cast-iron skillet, but this takes practice. For those who want a more controlled experience (or if you're frying for a crowd of hundreds, as I often do), I recommend using an electric deep fryer (preferably Waring models, which are no joke some of the best a home cook can get). Still, deep-fat fryers do have dangerous traits. For instance, keep an eye on the electrical cord. Don't leave it where something might snag it, and dump the load of hot oil (one reason I prefer the Waring brand of deep fryers is that they have breakaway magnetic safety cords). Also, be careful whenever you add food to a deep-fat fryer. If food gets dumped in too suddenly, if the fat is too hot, or

if there are pockets of liquid in the prepared food, the hot fat can spray. Because a lot of foods contain moisture, grease splatters are not uncommon, so always wear gloves, don't put your face anywhere near the hot oil, and be on guard for those splatters.

USE THE RIGHT OIL

Always follow the recipe instructions with heating oil to achieve the proper temperature. To ensure fewer chances of grease fires and for evenly cooked foods you should use an oil with a high smoke point (the higher the smoke point, the higher you can heat the oil before it burns). Fats with high smoke points include safflower oil, peanut oil, canola oil, lard, and duck fat.

TO DISPOSE OF COOKING OIL

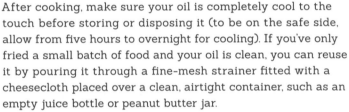

After cooking, make sure your oil is completely cool to the touch before storing or disposing it (to be on the safe side, allow from five hours to overnight for cooling). If you've only fried a small batch of food and your oil is clean, you can reuse it by pouring it through a fine-mesh strainer fitted with a cheesecloth placed over a clean, airtight container, such as an empty juice bottle or peanut butter jar.

When disposing of your oil, whatever you do, NEVER, EVER pour it down a drain or toilet. If you do, you will destroy your plumbing. One easy method is to freeze it first by pouring it into a 1-gallon Ziploc® bag and then placing that in another Ziploc. Take care to close the bags securely to guard against leaks. Freeze and then toss.

When I need to get rid of my oil, I use an Eco-fresh, yo! Japanese product called Katamete-pon. It's a powder that congeals used oil into a solid brick of fat, making for an effortless, eco-friendly disposal. You can even compost the brick of fat, as long as the oil wasn't used to cook meat. It's available online and in most Chinatowns and Asian markets across the United States and the EU.

And if you happen to live near a biodiesel company that makes diesel fuel from used cooking grease, give them a call and see if they want your old oil. Many biodiesel companies will pick up used oil right from your crib, saving you the hassle.

HOW TO HANDLE YOUR MEAT! (AND OTHER POINTERS)

I assume you know the basics about handling raw flesh, but just in case, here we go. First, be sure to wash your hands in warm, soapy water (I always use food handlers' gloves when working with flesh). Next, keep raw meat, poultry, and fish and their juices away from other food. For example, after cutting up any of the three, wash your hands, the knife, and the cutting board in hot, soapy water before using the knife and board to dice veggies or any other food items. Better yet, keep a set of separate knives and cutting boards for raw meat.

For safe cooking, always follow the recipe instructions regarding cooked meats' internal temperatures. (For more on food safety, consult the USDA online food safety guidelines.)

Note that kitchen towels, sponges, and cloths can all harbor bacteria, especially after cleaning up meat juices. Wash them often and replace sponges every few weeks. To sanitize sponges, bring a large pot of water to boil. Toss the sponges into a large, heatproof bowl along with a capful of bleach, pour boiling water on top, and let them sit for three to five minutes. Strain and rinse the sponges with cool water. I do this once a week. Always squeeze your sponges dry and store them in a dry place.

Other tips: thaw food in the microwave or in the refrigerator. DO NOT thaw items on the kitchen counter. This allows bacteria to grow in the outer layers of the food before the inside thaws. If you plan to marinate or brine meat, do it in the refrigerator, too.

For cleanup, always wash your work area with soap and hot water, and then go over it with a disinfectant or citrus-based, eco-friendly cleaning product. I squeeze half a lemon over all surfaces, including my cutting boards, and then scrub everything with the lemon, cut side down. Dry the surface with paper towels or a clean cloth.

SETTING UP
A SMOKER

I'm guessing a lot of you didn't grow up with home-rigged barrel smokers rolling 24/7 in the backyard like I did. You might think that smoking is a massive pain in the ass, for old-timers only. But trust me, smoking meats (or fish or even cheese!) in the proper way—slow and low—imparts flavors that liquid smoke just can't touch, and it's not that hard. You don't even have to buy an expensive set-up to get it right. Seriously, all you need is a little DFC smoking science and a standard charcoal BBQ grill with a shutdown cover. It's all about cooking with indirect heat, where your meats aren't blazed directly on top of the coals.

So look at your BBQ grill and imagine it split in half vertically, right down the middle. On one side make a heap of coals and light them up. Get this roaring and let the flames settle down until the coals are glowing white. On the other side, next to the coals, place a metal (foil is fine) heat-resistant pan filled with water. The water helps control the heat and adds moisture to the system. Then lower the lid, leaving it open slightly by propping it up with the grates (which helps with the air flow). Use a digital thermometer to check when the grill reaches 225°F.

Just before you hit that perfect number, grab a big handful of fragrant wood chips (such as maple, mesquite, or hickory) and woody herbs (rosemary's a good one), lift the grate, and throw them onto your coals. Put the grate back in place and lay your meat on the side over the water pan—not over the hot, smoking coals. (Note that you can also add a pan of water on the grill, over the coal side, for added humidity and temperature control.) Replace the lid, and look at that: you're smashing it with indirect cooking! Let the meat do its magical business for the desired amount of time, per the recipe. That's Slow Skool at its best.

DANTE FRIED CHICKEN
A VARIETY COOKING SHOW
LIVEMUSIC
RYE RYE (BALTIMORE, US)
SEPT. 6TH
RESTURANG
LJUNGGREN/
BRUNOGALLERIAN
D.J.
PRINCE GLAESER
JOHANNA B
TURKDISCO
SPECIAL SOUTHERN
STYLE DRINK MENU
AKUSTISKA LIVE
FRAMTRÄDANDEN
SLOWJAMS
K.F.C. R.I.P.

WHOLE WORLD FRIED CHICKEN!

CHAPTER 1

I was seven years old when I first tried my hand at cooking. I'd seen fried chicken made countless times, so I figured, why not? But the first time I tried it, well, I went and burned the kitchen floor right up! The problem was the old stove—I could barely reach it and it didn't ignite automatically, so I lit some newspaper that immediately collapsed in my hand. I rushed to the bathroom to get water, but by the time I'd gotten back half of the kitchen's linoleum floor was on fire. Damn, I got my whoopings that summer from many different family members: my grandmother, my father, my aunt, my uncles. But that didn't do anything to stop my love for cooking.

My passion for food stayed with me on into college, where I studied anthropology and began to deconstruct the multicultural cooking of my childhood. I found it fascinating that different cultures borrowed so many culinary customs from each other, in large part thanks to the spice trade that used to rule the world. Spices were more valuable than gold! I came to realize that food really is a cross-cultural educational tool.

Did you know that the first recorded deep frying of a chicken was in Asia? That's right, the Chinese were the first to take meats and boil them in oil. It may not have been the Southern Heritage fried chicken that we've come to love in the United States, but the Chinese were nonetheless pioneers. I thank them for introducing us to a technique that would later morph into my own, updated version of the classic dish.

ROY CHOI &
ROADSTOVES

The incredible chef Roy Choi was instrumental in kick-starting the new wave of gourmet food trucks in LA when he partnered with the company Roadstoves to create Kogi BBQ truck. It started when Roadstoves developed a concept to lease vehicles to vendors for the purpose of creating high-end artisanal food trucks (and help guide them through the daunting process of mobile food vending), and leased one to Roy, a friend of mine. Roadstoves helped us get up and running as well. The new gourmet food trucks are an important part of migrant food culture in America, and Roy brought a whole new game and flavor to the mix. A lot has already been written about Kogi BBQ and the fact that Roy was a pioneer who believed in cross-cultural education between Mexican and Korean cultures. He also brought social networking to the food truck scene in a huge way—he was responsible for the Twitter truck craze. Roy's efforts have been vital to the LA community—together, Mexican and Korean cultures are the embodiment of California lovin'.

The DFC Ride or Fry truck at a Roadstoves event in Los Angeles, CA.

¢REDIT CRUNCH FRIED CHICKEN
AKA JEAN'S SOCK-IT-TO-ME FRIED CHICKEN

This signature recipe spans three generations of women (and a couple of men) in my family, each of whom added her own flip to it. The story starts way back in the Great Depression, when nothing went to waste. That explains the origins of the DFC crust: my elders would ground up stale bread crumbs, leftover nuts, old crackers, oats, and cereals—aka "the bits"—and add that to flour. My bits nowadays boast thirty-somethin' ingredients, including fresh herbs and spices, which combine to create a unique texture and flavor. That's the outside. On the inside, the chicken gets its tenderness and flavor from soaking it in buttermilk and lemon zest for hours. Now, you know I can't hand out my own secret recipe just like that (is you CRAZY?!) but rejoice, as I've given you the incredible bootleg version right here. (By the way, the bits are a personal thing—see sidebar for how to make your own custom version.)

SERVES **6 as an entrée or 8 tapas style**

PREP AND COOKING TIME **1 hour, 20 minutes, plus 6 hours to overnight marinating**

4 boneless skinless chicken breasts
4 boneless skinless chicken thighs
1 gallon high-smoke-point oil, such as peanut, canola, or safflower

MARINADE

1½ cups buttermilk
1 pinch paprika
1 pinch garlic powder
1 pinch onion powder
Zest of one lemon

DRY BATTER

1 cup potato starch or 4 tsps. cornstarch
3 cups all-purpose flour
½ cup yellow cornmeal
1 to 2 tbsps. salt
½ cup Fried Chicken Spice Mix (page 190)
1 tbsp. chopped fresh rosemary leaves
1 to 2 tbsps. minced fresh basil
1 to 3 cups bits (page 193), depending on how crunchy you like it

WET BATTER

2 eggs
1 cup buttermilk
½ to 1 cup beer (whatever kind you like)
Sriracha

SPECIAL EQUIPMENT

Candy thermometer
Meat thermometer

MARINATE THE CHICKEN

1. Cut the chicken pieces lengthwise into ½-inch strips.
2. In a large bowl, combine the buttermilk, spices, and lemon zest. Add the chicken and toss to coat. Cover and refrigerate for 6 to 24 hours.

↪

MAKE THE DRY BATTER

1. When the chicken is almost ready to come out of the fridge, mix together in a medium bowl the potato or cornstarch, flour, cornmeal, and all the dry batter spices except for the rosemary, basil, and bits.
2. Pour half of the flour mixture into a large bowl.
3. Add the rosemary, basil, and bits to the remaining flour in a second large bowl.

MAKE THE WET BATTER

In a large bowl, combine all wet batter ingredients. The consistency should be slightly runny but still have a slight creaminess to it. Add more beer if batter is too thick.

COAT THE CHICKEN

1. Before you start breading and frying, set up your work area. See Get Set Up sidebar on opposite page.
2. Remove the chicken from the marinade, shake off excess liquid, and pat dry.
3. In small batches, add chicken pieces to the first bowl filled with flour mixture, making sure to coat each piece. Set floured chicken pieces on the newspaper or wire racks.
4. Using one hand, dip floured chicken pieces into the wet batter and shake off excess.

ALL ABOUT
THE BITS

My grandmother came from an era where nothing went to waste, not even the ends of onions or garlic skins, which were always kept and used for stock. The "bits" for fried chicken coating followed suit—my grandmother would collect day-old bread or bagels from bakers and keep them in a big-ass container until she was ready to grind them up and add the crumbs to her flour. The original Credit Crunch/Sock-It-to-Me Fried Chicken recipe used ground oat seeds, leftover cornbread, biscuits, and the aforementioned bread and bagels. I try to keep the bits neutral, for the most part, by using things like dried cereals, oats, and any type of nuts. Starting with the basic formula for Bits (page 193), experiment with your own mixture of ingredients. Just keep in mind that the bits affect the flavor of the overall dish, which is why I avoid stronger-flavored breads such as rye.

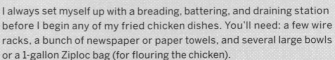

GET SET UP

I always set myself up with a breading, battering, and draining station before I begin any of my fried chicken dishes. You'll need: a few wire racks, a bunch of newspaper or paper towels, and several large bowls or a 1-gallon Ziploc bag (for flouring the chicken).

Cover your entire work area in newspaper to protect against bacteria, and also for easy cleanup, and place the wire racks over the paper. Place the bowls (or bag) of dry and wet batter and coating in the order you'll use them next to the newspapers. After you apply the bread coating (the last step), place the chicken on the wire racks or directly on the newspaper to let the crust set before frying. This ensures a crust that sticks, and you'll lose less flour and bits in your cooking oil, which can degrade the oil. You will use the same racks and newspaper to drain the fried chicken after it comes out of the oil.

5. With your other (dry) hand, dig a little grave in flour-and-bits mixture in the second bowl, place chicken in it, then bury to coat, pressing down firmly. Gently lift chicken, shaking off excess coating. After three pieces are coated, take a fork and toss the flour around to break up any clumps in the bowl. Do this every so often to help keep the flour from gluing up and becoming unusable.

6. Place breaded chicks on wire racks set in a baking sheet or over newspaper. Let sit for 20 minutes to set the crust.

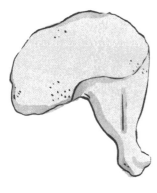

FRY THE CHICKEN

1. Meanwhile, prepare your deep fryer according to the instructions or fill a heavy-bottomed, high-sided 12-inch frying pan (preferably cast-iron) or 6-quart Dutch oven about halfway to three-quarters full with oil. Heat on medium-high to 325°F to 350°F.

2. Working in batches, fry the chicken pieces about 3 to 4 minutes per side, until deep golden brown and the internal temperature reads 165°F.

3. Using tongs, remove fried chicken from oil and place on a wire rack, newspaper, or paper towels to drain. Serve with Coconut Honey Biscuits (page 172) and Apricot Crack Sauce (page 202) for the ultimate DFC dish.

JUKE ISLAND CURRY WINGS

When I talk about about family recipes, I'm really talking about the energy, love, and positivity that goes into the food. My Aunt Novia added a lot of love to her incredible wing recipe, and you could taste it. This Aunt Novia–inspired hot curry spice blend is full-on Louisiana-meets-Jamaica. A marinade of buttermilk and pineapple juice adds an extra flavor dimension, along with the insanely crunchy crust made from yucca and shaved coconut. These wings are perfect with a splash of Sriracha.

SERVES **6 as an entrée or 8 tapas style**   PREP AND COOKING TIME **1 hour, plus 3 hours to overnight marinating**

4 lbs. chicken wings, split at the joints and tips discarded
1 gallon high-smoke-point oil, such as peanut or canola

CURRY MARINADE
2 tbsps. olive oil
1 small onion, chopped
1 tsp. chopped fresh ginger
1 tsp. chopped garlic
1 bay leaf
1 Scotch bonnet pepper, ribs and seeds removed, diced
1 20-oz. can of crushed pineapple in juice

1 cup coconut milk
1 cup coconut water
1 cinnamon stick
2 tbsps. curry powder
1 tsp. cumin
1 tsp. turmeric
¼ tsp. black peppercorns, crushed
2 large eggs, beaten
1 cup buttermilk

DRY BATTER
2 cups all-purpose flour
1 cup white cornmeal

2 tbsps. cornstarch
1 tbsp. All-Purpose Chicken Spice (page 190) or other seasoned salt
2 pinches white pepper, or more to taste
1 yucca, shredded and chopped into a small dice
1 cup unsweetened coconut flakes, coarsely chopped

SPECIAL EQUIPMENT
Candy thermometer
Meat thermometer

MARINATE THE CHICKEN

1. In a medium sauce pan set on medium to high, sauté the onion and ginger in olive oil until fragrant and soft, about 5 minutes. Add the garlic and bay leaf and cook for another minute or two. Add the hot pepper and pineapple and pineapple juice and simmer for 2 minutes. Then add the coconut milk and the coconut water. Reduce heat to low and continue to simmer while doing next step.

2. In a small pan set on medium, toast the cinnamon stick, moving it around in the pan frequently, until fragrant and slightly smoking, about 5 minutes. Add the cinnamon stick to the pineapple mixture.

3. In the same pan, add the curry, cumin, turmeric, and peppercorns, stirring constantly. Remove pan from heat when it starts to smoke and become fragrant, about 2 minutes. Add spice mixture to pineapple mixture and simmer on low for 20 to 30 minutes.

THE FLOUR

The base ingredients that I roll with for my seasoned flours are salt, black and white pepper, onion and garlic powder, and paprika. After adding those, you can carefully mix in other spices to taste. As for fresh herbs, I always use basil and rosemary, because I like the way they taste when they're fried. Fresh sage pops too. Dry herbs like oregano and ground bay leaves are great too, but for me, as long as you have fresh rosemary and basil, you're good. For more on flour spice mixes, see pages 192–193.

When frying, the trick with the flour is to add some sort of starch or baking powder to the mix, which will give your crust extra crispiness. It also acts as a binding agent, so when you rest the chicken (which you should do for at least 15 minutes before frying) the crust will adhere nicely to the meat.

4. Transfer sauce to a medium bowl to cool. Once cool, discard the cinnamon stick and bay leaf. Pour the mixture into a blender, and pulse a few times for a coarse purée. It's better a little chunky.
5. Pour mixture back into a bowl. Whisk in the eggs and the dairy.
6. Place wings in a large bowl or casserole dish, and pour curry pineapple mixture over the chicken. Soak for 3 hours or up to overnight, covered and refrigerated, periodically jostling the wings to evenly distribute the flavors.

MAKE THE DRY BATTER
1. Remove container of marinated wings from fridge and set aside to reach room temperature.
2. Meanwhile, combine the flour, cornmeal, cornstarch, seasoned salt, and white pepper in a large bowl. Add the yucca and coconut, stirring to combine. Set aside.

COAT THE CHICKEN
1. Before you start breading and frying, set up your work area. See Get Set Up on page 33 for instructions.
2. Remove the wings from marinade and shake off excess liquid.
3. Coat each wing in the flour-yucca mixture by digging a grave and burying the chicken, then gently lifting and shaking off excess breading. After three wings are coated, take a fork and toss the flour around to break up any clumps in the bowl. Do this every so often to help keep the flour from gluing up and becoming unusable.
4. Let the wings rest on a wire rack for 15 minutes to set the crust.

FRY THE CHICKEN
1. Meanwhile, prepare your deep fryer according to the instructions or fill a heavy-bottomed, high-sided 12-inch frying pan (preferably cast iron) or 6-quart Dutch oven about halfway to three-quarters full with oil. Heat on medium-high to 325°F to 350°F.
2. Working in batches, place several wings in oil and cook for 8 to 10 minutes, until crispy and browned and internal temperature is 165°F. I serve these as they are or with Sriracha.

PEACH!-N-PECAN WINGS

Everybody loves chicken wings, whether fried, baked, or barbecued. But there's one thing I need from my wings—they gotta be falling-off-the-bone tender. And they can't have soggy skin—I *hate* that! *Pssst* . . . I'll let you in on the secret for making tender, crispy wings: first smoke them, then deep fry them, and *then* toss them in BBQ sauce. Just like with hot wings, you only need to fry them for one minute to get them crispy. These wings make you want to suck and gnaw on the bones, and that's the way I like it!

SERVES **4 as an entrée or 6 tapas style**　　PREP AND COOKING TIME **2 hours, plus 3 hours to overnight marinating**

16 chicken wings, split at the
　joints and tips discarded
2　tbsps. olive oil
1½ cups apple or cherry
　wood chips
1　gallon high-smoke-point oil,
　such as peanut or canola

RUB

1　cup dark brown sugar,
　firmly packed
½ cup sweet paprika
¼ cup kosher salt
⅛ cup garlic powder
2　tbsps. freshly ground
　black pepper

1　tbsp. poultry seasoning
2　tbsps. ground ginger
2　tbsps. onion powder
2　tsps. dried rosemary,
　crushed with your fingers

SAUCE

2　garlic cloves, peeled
2　red bell peppers, ribs and
　seeds removed, halved
1　tbsp. unsalted butter
½ cup whiskey
½ cup water
2　tbsps. Sriracha
2　tbsps. molasses

4　tbsps. ketchup
　A pinch of kosher or sea salt
½ cup roasted pecans,
　finely crushed
½ cup dried cherries
2 fresh peaches, blanched, skin
　removed, pitted, and diced
1　8-oz. can of crushed
　pineapple

SPECIAL EQUIPMENT

Smoker or grill set for smoking
(see pages 24–25)
Oven thermometer
Candy thermometer
Meat thermometer

SPICE THE CHICKEN

1. In a small bowl combine all the ingredients for the rub.
2. Coat the chicken with olive oil and then add the rub. Toss to coat. Cover with plastic film and refrigerate for 3 hours or overnight.

SMOKE THE CHICKEN

1. When ready to smoke the wings, put the wood chips in your grill and prepare direct and indirect heating zones (see pages 24–25 for setup instructions).
2. Preheat grill to 300°F to 315°F. Use oven thermometer to accurately gauge temperature.
3. While grill is preheating, put the garlic in a foil pouch, and poke a hole in it.

BAKE THAT CHICKEN

As an alternative to deep frying the chicken in any of my fried chicken recipes, you can bake it with only a slight adjustment to the instructions. Just take this one extra step: when the pieces are racked and drying, fill up a spray bottle with peanut oil and saturate them with a few pumps of the oil. Then pop them in the oven on a rack set over a baking sheet at 350°F until golden brown, about 20 to 30 minutes, depending on the thickness of the chicken pieces. The texture will be slightly different to the fried chicken but still damn delicious.

4. Put wings and the garlic pouch on the indirect heat side of the grill, close the lid, and smoke them for 35 minutes.
5. Take the pouch off the grill and set aside. The roasted garlic will go in the sauce.
6. Rotate wings and continue smoking for another 30 to 35 minutes. The wings are done when internal temperature hits 165°F (avoid the bone when poking them with thermometer).

MAKE THE SAUCE

1. Turn on all four stove burners to low and place the pepper halves, skin side down, directly over the flame. Roast for a few minutes, rotating the peppers with a pair of tongs until as much of the skin as possible is blistered and blackened. Transfer peppers to a glass bowl until cool enough to handle. Remove as much of the skin as you can.
2. Put bell peppers, roasted garlic (squeezed out of the skin), butter, whiskey, and water into a blender and purée until smooth. Add the Sriracha, molasses, ketchup, and salt, then liquefy. Taste and adjust the flavors to your preference. Add more Sriracha if you want it hotter, or more molasses if you want it sweeter.
3. Transfer sauce to a small sauce pan over low, and add the pecans, cherries, and pineapple. Cook for 10 to 15 minutes. Keep sauce warm.

REUSE THAT OIL

Hold up on chucking that frying oil. It's still usable, so save it cuz it has a nice smoked flavor that will enhance anything else you fry in it.

FRY THE CHICKEN

1. Before you start frying, set up your draining station. See Get Set Up on page 33 for tips.
2. Prepare your deep fryer according to the instructions or fill a heavy-bottomed, high-sided 12-inch frying pan (preferably cast-iron) or 6-quart Dutch oven about halfway to three-quarters full with oil. Heat on medium-high to 325°F to 350°F.
3. Working in batches, fry the wings for 1 minute per batch. Set the fried wings on the wire racks over newspaper to drain.
4. When the wings have cooled but are still warm, toss them in a large bowl with half of the warm sauce, adding more sauce if you like. Unused sauce will keep, refrigerated in an airtight container, for 1 week.

LA RAZA FRIED CHICKEN

¡QUE VIVA!

This chicken reflects the food I grew up with: it combines the all-American experience (fried chicken) with the influences of Mexican culture, which was a huge part of my upbringing. The inspiration for it grew from one time when I was cooking at an Adidas party with my friend Miguel Mendez, a singer-songwriter. Miguel taught me this cool brining technique, which he learned from his grandmother, and I used the technique to create what I call La Raza Fried Chicken. The torn corn tortillas and rich Mexican and Cajun spices blend together to create a unique Creole-style Cinco de Mayo for your mouth.

SERVES **6 as an entrée or 10 tapas style**   PREP AND COOKING TIME **45 minutes, plus overnight brining**

4   pieces boneless
    skinless chicken breast
4   boneless skinless
    chicken thighs
1   gallon high-smoke-point oil,
    such as peanut, canola,
    or safflower

BRINE
3   cups brewed black tea
1   tsp. salt
4   bay leaves
1   tsp. dried oregano
    Zest of 1 large orange
    A pinch of Spanish paprika
3   garlic cloves, chopped

½   small yellow onion, quartered
2   cups buttermilk

WET BATTER
3   chipotle peppers *en adobo*,
    plus 2 tsps. adobo sauce
3   large eggs
2   cups buttermilk

DRY COATING
3   tortillas (red, yellow, blue, green,
    or plain—I like to mix the colors)
3   cups all-purpose flour
1   cup white cornmeal
2   tsps. tapioca powder
2   tbsps. garlic powder

2   tbsps. onion powder
4   tsps. Spanish paprika
2   tsps. ground cumin
2   tsps. celery seed
    A pinch of white pepper
1   tsp. dried oregano
2   to 3 tsps. sea salt
½   tsp. freshly ground black pepper
½   cup sesame seeds
6   sprigs fresh cilantro or parsley

SPECIAL EQUIPMENT
    Candy thermometer

BRINE THE CHICKEN

1. Cut each chicken breast lengthwise into 3 equal pieces, then cut each piece crosswise into 8 pieces, for a total of 24 pieces. Halve chicken thighs for a total of 8 pieces.
2. Combine all brine ingredients except the buttermilk in a large stock pot. Cover, bring to a boil for 1 minute, and remove from heat. Transfer to a large bowl and let cool completely. Stir in the buttermilk.
3. Submerge the chicken pieces in the brine. Cover and refrigerate for 12 to 24 hours.

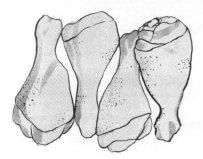

MAKE THE WET BATTER

In a blender, purée the chipotle peppers and adobo sauce, eggs, and wet-batter buttermilk. Scrape into a small bowl.

MAKE THE DRY COATING

1. In a food processor, finely chop the tortillas, but don't turn them into dust!
2. In a large bowl, combine the flour, cornmeal, tapioca, garlic, and onion powders, paprika, cumin, celery seed, white pepper, oregano, salt, and pepper. Transfer half of the mixture to a second bowl.
3. Add the tortilla crumbs, sesame seeds, and chopped cilantro to the second bowl.

COAT THE CHICKEN

1. Before you start breading and frying, set up your work area. See Get Set Up (page 33) for instructions.
2. Remove the chicken from the brine, shake off excess liquid, and pat dry.
3. In small batches, add chicken pieces to the first bowl to coat with flour mixture. Set floured chicken pieces on the newspaper or wire racks.
4. Using one hand, dip floured chicken pieces into the wet batter and shake off excess.
5. With your other (dry) hand, dig a little grave in the dry coating in the second bowl, place chicken in it, then bury to coat, pressing down firmly. Gently lift chicken, shaking off excess coating. After three pieces are coated, take a fork and toss the flour around to break up any clumps in the bowl. Do this every so often to help keep the flour from gluing up and becoming unusable.
6. Place coated chicken on wire racks set in a baking sheet or over newspaper. Let sit for 20 minutes to set the crust.

FRY THE CHICKEN

1. Meanwhile, prepare your deep fryer according to the instructions or fill a heavy-bottomed, high-sided 12-inch frying pan (preferably cast-iron) or 6-quart Dutch oven about halfway to three-quarters full with oil. Place a crushed garlic clove (skin still on) and some onion scraps in the oil. Heat on medium-high to 325°F to 350°F.
2. Once oil is heated, fish out the garlic and onion with a slotted spoon and discard.
3. Working in batches, fry the chicken pieces about 4 to 5 minutes per side, until deep golden brown and the internal temperature reads 165°F.
4. Using tongs, carefully remove the chicken pieces from the oil, and place them on a tray lined with paper towels, a cooling rack, or newspaper. Let the chicken cool a bit before serving. I love this dish with fresh chili paste. See Yo Allah Fried Chicken (opposite page) for an easy chili paste recipe.

YO ALLAH FRIED CHICKEN
AND PICKLED CUCUMBERS

Yo, even if it's those Trader Joe's frozen dinners, I eat Indian food at least once a week without fail. I love the Indian culture's celebration of spices—the region was a major destination in the spice trade, which during the Middle Ages was dominated by Muslim merchants who sailed the Indian Ocean. Because of the spice business, the countries of the Near and Far East were brought into contact with European nations. This recipe is a shout-out to the spices, spirituality, and food that bound all those countries together.

SERVES **6 as an entrée or 10 tapas style**   PREP AND COOKING TIME **1 hour, plus 6 hours to overnight brining**

4 boneless skinless chicken breasts, cut in half and butterflied
4 boneless skinless chicken thighs, halved
1 high-smoke-point oil, such as peanut, canola, or safflower

BRINE
1 tsp. ground ginger
1 tsp. ground cumin
1 tsp. ground coriander
1 tsp. paprika
1 tsp. turmeric
1 tsp. salt
1 tsp. cayenne pepper
1½ cups buttermilk
1 cup water

PICKLED CUCUMBERS
¼ cup water
¾ cup white vinegar
⅓ cup white sugar
¼ cup finely chopped fresh parsley
¾ tsp. sea salt
⅛ tsp. freshly ground black pepper
4 medium cucumbers, peeled and thinly sliced

WET BATTER
12 dried red chili peppers
3 garlic cloves, minced
½ tsp. salt
2 tbsps. olive oil
1 tsp. ground coriander
1 tsp. ground caraway seeds
½ tsp. ground cumin
2 large eggs, lightly beaten
1 cup plain yogurt

DRY BATTER
3 cups all-purpose flour
2 tsps. baking powder
½ cup white cornmeal
1 cup potato starch or cornstarch
2 tbsps. salt
1 tbsp. cayenne pepper
1 tsp. ground cumin or seeds
1 tsp. coriander seeds
1 to 2 tbsps. granulated garlic
1 tbsp. granulated onion
1 tbsp. celery seed
1 handful cilantro leaves, minced
1 cup pistachios, shelled and crushed
1 cup day-old or dry-baked naan, processed into crumbs

BRINE THE CHICKEN
1. Cut the chicken lengthwise into 1-inch strips.
2. In a small bowl, combine the ginger, cumin, coriander, paprika, turmeric, salt, and cayenne pepper.

3. Heat a small sauce pan on medium and add the spice mixture. Toast until fragrant, about 2 to 3 minutes.

4. Transfer toasted spices to a blender. Add the buttermilk and water, and purée.

5. In a bowl, combine the chicken with the brine. Cover and refrigerate 6 hours or overnight.

MAKE THE PICKLED CUCUMBERS

In large bowl, combine the water, vinegar, sugar, parsley, salt, and pepper. Add the cucumbers and toss well. Place mixture into an airtight container and refrigerate at least 3 hours or overnight.

MAKE THE WET BATTER

1. Soak the dried chilies in hot water for 30 minutes. Drain chilies and remove stems and seeds.

2. In a food processor, combine the soaked chilies, garlic, salt, and olive oil. Add the coriander, caraway, and cumin, and blend to a smooth paste.

3. In a small bowl, combine 1 heaping tablespoon of the chili paste with the eggs and yogurt. If the consistency is too thick, add a few tablespoons of water to loosen the mixture. See Save Your Chili Paste for storage information.

SAVE YOUR CHILI PASTE

The remaining chili paste can be used as a condiment for any dish in need of some flavor and heat. To store, top it with olive oil and keep in the fridge in an airtight container for up to two weeks.

MAKE THE DRY BATTER

1. In a large bowl, combine all dry batter ingredients except for the cilantro, pistachios, and naan breadcrumbs.

2. Put half the flour mixture along with the cilantro, pistachios, and naan breadcrumbs into a second large bowl.

COAT THE CHICKEN

1. Before you start breading and frying, set up your work area. See Get Set Up (page 33) for instructions.

2. Remove the chicken from the brine, shake off excess liquid, and pat dry.

WASH UP

ALWAYS wash your hands with hot water and loads of soap when handling flesh. I use food handlers' gloves when handling meats. Always wash your prep area with soap and hot water, and then go over it with a disinfectant. Don't want the chemicals? Take half a lemon, squeeze the juice onto your work surface, and use the cut side of the lemon to scrub the area. Let the juice sit for 3 minutes and then wipe with a paper towel.

BRINING AND MARINATING

There are a lot of different brining and marinating mixtures, which are used primarily to tenderize the meat and add flavor. A brine is a solution of water (or another liquid) and salt (and sometimes sugar and other spices), and a marinade can be a mixture of many different things but usually has an acid, like lemon juice or vinegar. For chicken, I like to use a marinade made with dairy, such as buttermilk, yogurt, or cottage cheese. Any marinade with cultured dairy will add a creaminess to the chicken that brines won't. Whether brining or marinating, submerge the meat and soak it for at least 6 hours in the refrigerator to ensure maximum tenderness and flavor. Overnight is perfect. I've even brined for 2 days, and the chicken literally melts in your mouth when cooked. If you're short on time, 1 hour is better than nothing.

3. In small batches, add chicken pieces to the first bowl to coat with flour mixture. Set floured chicken pieces on the newspaper or wire racks. Transfer any leftover flour mixture to the second large bowl containing the breadcrumbs, and stir to combine.
4. Using one hand, dip floured chicken pieces into the chili-egg batter and shake off excess.
5. With your other (dry) hand, dig a little grave in the dry coating in the second bowl, place chicken in it, then bury to coat, pressing down firmly. Gently lift chicken, shaking off excess coating. After three pieces are coated, take a fork and toss the flour around to break up any clumps in the bowl. Do this every so often to help keep the flour from gluing up and becoming unusable.
6. Place coated chicken on wire racks set in a baking sheet or over newspaper. Let sit for 20 minutes to set the crust.

FRY THE CHICKEN

1. Meanwhile, prepare your deep fryer according to the instructions or fill a heavy-bottomed, high-sided 12-inch frying pan (preferably cast-iron) or 6-quart Dutch oven about halfway to three-quarters full with oil. Heat on medium-high to 325°F to 350°F.
2. Working in batches, fry the chicken pieces until golden brown, about 3 to 4 minutes per side. The internal temperature should read 165°F.
3. Using tongs, carefully remove fried chicken from the oil and place on a wire rack, newspaper, or paper towels to drain. Serve the Yo Allah with Pickled Cucumbers and plain yogurt. This dish is very spicy; no need for extra hot sauce.

APRICOT-CASHEW HOT WINGS

I cooked up these wings with dubstep don and electronic music pioneer Rusko at London's infamous, annual Notting Hill Carnival. Now Rusko, who relocated from the UK to LA, says I've ruined hot wings for him by setting the bar so high! My wings are glazed in a variation of my signature sweet-and-spicy Apricot Crack Sauce and hit with toasted, crushed cashews. Feel free to improvise with different dried fruits and preserves, such as peaches or pineapple, to change up the fruit flavors. And stay away from monster wings for this one—small ones are much better, preferably organic or pasture raised.

SERVES **8 as an entrée or 12 tapas style**   PREP AND COOKING TIME **1½ hours, plus 3 hours overnight for marinating**

5 lbs. small chicken wings, tips removed and split at the joint
1 gallon high-smoke-point oil, such as peanut or canola

MARINADE
2 cups buttermilk
2 squirts Sriracha

SAUCE
½ cup (1 stick) unsalted butter
2 tbsps. red pepper flakes

1 5-oz. bottle of your favorite hot sauce
4 squirts Sriracha
1 cup apricot preserves
1 cup cashews, crushed
¼ cup chopped dried apricots
2 or 3 jalapeños or your favorite chili, ribs and seeds removed, diced
1 thumb-size piece of fresh ginger, peeled and coarsely chopped

COATING
1 cup yellow cornmeal
2 cups all-purpose flour
1 cup cashews, finely crushed
¼ cup All-Purpose Chicken Spice (page 190)

WET BATTER
2 large eggs
½ cup water or beer

SPECIAL EQUIPMENT
Candy thermometer
Meat thermometer

MARINATE THE CHICKEN
1. Rinse the chicken wings and pat them dry with paper towels.
2. In a large bowl, combine the buttermilk and Sriracha. Add the wings, cover with plastic wrap, and refrigerate for 3 hours to 24 hours.

MAKE THE SAUCE
In a 10-inch skillet set on low, heat the butter, chili flakes, hot sauce, and Sriracha. Add the apricot preserves, cashews, dried apricots, jalapeños, and ginger, stirring to combine. Simmer on low for 10 minutes. Keep warm.

MAKE THE DRY COATING
In a large bowl, combine all dry coating ingredients.

The annual Notting Hill rager was thrown by Mad Decent (the record label) and sponsored by Red Bull in 2009. I cooked up with a grip of fun people, including Rusko, Major Lazer, Toddla T, and Maluca. This gigantic Caribbean carnival perfectly reflects what Transatlantic African food is all about! We fed 1,500 mouths, the most I have cooked for, ever. We smoked something like 220 pounds of pork shoulder and fried up around 200 pounds of chicken. It was crazy! That year we were commissioned by Red Bull to shoot an episode of *The Dante Fried Chicken Show* about the experience. So I had to play the role of celebrity chef in front of the camera, which is not me at all. The only thing that got me through that day was my boy TFC—AKA Terence Teh. And of course the eighteen-year-old bottle of Jameson on the shoot. You probably can't tell on the video, but I was feelin' it!

Dante with Rusko
in an early cook UP

MAKE THE WET BATTER
In a small bowl, lightly beat the egg and water or beer.

COAT THE WINGS
1. Before you start breading and frying, set up your work area. See Get Set Up (page 33) for instructions.
2. Remove the chicken from the marinade, shake off excess liquid, and pat dry.
3. Working in batches, dip the wings in egg wash, shaking off excess.
4. Dunk the wings into the flour mixture, shaking off excess coating. Every so often toss the flour with a fork to help keep the flour from gluing up and becoming unusable.
5. Place coated wings on a wire rack set inside a baking sheet. Let the wings sit for 15 minutes to set the crust before frying.

FRY THE WINGS
1. Meanwhile, prepare your deep fryer according to the instructions or fill a heavy-bottomed, high-sided 12-inch frying pan (preferably cast-iron) or 6-quart Dutch oven about halfway to three-quarters full with oil. Heat on medium-high to 325°F to 350°F.
2. Working in batches, fry the wings until deep golden brown, about 8 to 10 minutes, turning them halfway through. The internal temperature of the wings should be 165°F; avoid the bone when poking them with the thermometer.
3. Remove fried wings from oil with tongs and set them on wire racks over newspaper to drain.
4. When the wings have drained but are still hot, use a clean set of tongs to drop the wings into the warm apricot sauce and evenly coat them. Place the wings on a baking baking sheet lined with foil; if you're not ready to serve, keep them in the oven on its lowest setting. I like to serve 'em with Boujee Ranch Sauce (page 200).

HONEY-BAKED PISTACHIO WINGS

These are some seriously addictive jump-offs—people just can't get enough of them. The secret is to steam the wings, dry season the hell out of them, and then let them marinate overnight. The sweet and nutty sauce is the ultimate. Serve them up with good-old mashed potatoes and sautéed spinach, my favorite combo.

SERVES 4 as an entrée or 6 tapas style   PREP AND COOKING TIME **2 hours, plus 3 hours to overnight marinating**

16 whole chicken wings
2 tbsps. canola oil

RUB
½ cup sweet paprika
¼ cup sea salt
2 tbsps. garlic powder
2 tbsps. freshly ground black pepper

1 tbsp. All-Purpose Chicken Spice (page 190)
2 tbsps. ground ginger
2 tbsps. onion powder
2 tsps. dried rosemary, crushed with your fingers

SAUCE
3 tbsps. unsalted butter
1 garlic clove, minced
1 cup pistachios, toasted and finely crushed
1 cup honey
2 squirts Sriracha
½ tsp. sea salt

STEAM THE WINGS
1. Fill a 6-quart sauce pan fitted with a steamer basket with 1-inch of water. Bring to a boil.
2. Place the wings in the steamer basket, cover, reduce heat to medium. Steam the wings for 10 minutes.
3. Remove wings from basket and carefully pat them dry with paper towels.

SEASON THE CHICKEN
1. In a small bowl, combine the rub ingredients.
2. In a large bowl, coat wings with the oil, then add the rub and toss to coat well. Place coated wings a wire rack set in a baking sheet lined with paper towels, cover with plastic wrap, and refrigerate them for 3 hours or overnight.

BAKE THE WINGS
1. When ready to bake the wings, preheat oven to 425°F.
2. Replace the paper towels in the baking sheet with parchment paper. Return the racks to the baking sheets and put the wings in the middle rack of the oven.
3. Roast wings on the middle rack for 20 minutes. Turn them over and roast until the wings are cooked through and the skin is golden brown, another 20 minutes.

MAKE THE SAUCE

1. While the wings are baking, in an 8-inch pan set on medium, heat the butter, garlic, pistachios, and honey, until the butter and honey are melted and the sauce has combined, about 5 minutes.

2. Pour the sauce into a large bowl, then add the Sriracha and salt, stirring to combine.

GLAZE THE WINGS

When the wings are done, remove them from the oven. Using tongs, place the roasted wings into the sauce bowl and toss to coat. Serve warm.

!! WARNING: !!!
{TASTES-LIKE-CHICKEN}
{TOFU} NUGGETS

I encourage you to eat these tofu nuggets whether you consider yourself an herbivore, carnivore, or omnivore. Ask all the New Yorkers who ate them during the first eight years of DFC; the meat-eaters actually requested it instead of real chicken! For the best-quality tofu, I suggest buying from May Wah (see page 51); you can also look for veggie protein and/or mock chicken at premium health food stores like Whole Foods or any Asian supermarket.

SERVES **6; 10 tapas style**   PREP AND COOKING TIME **45 minutes, plus overnight marinating (optional)**

DRY COATING
¼ cup All-Purpose Chicken Spice (page 190)
1¼ cups all-purpose flour
1   cup Bits (page 193)
2   sprigs rosemary, stems discarded, leaves minced
3   sprigs basil, shredded

WET BATTER
2   cups soy milk
2   tbsps. white vinegar
3   tbsps. plain tofu yogurt
1   tsp. Sriracha
½   tsp. grated lemon zest

CHOOSE 1 PROTEIN:
2   lbs. flavored tofu nuggets, unbreaded, preferably May Wah (see page 51)

2   lbs. extra-firm unflavored tofu, cut into nuggets and marinated overnight (see Note)
2   lbs. mock meat suitable for breading and frying (see pages 198–199 for my seitan and tempeh recipes), cut into nuggets
½   gallon peanut oil

SPECIAL EQUIPMENT
Candy thermometer

MAKE THE DRY COATING
In a medium bowl, mix together the chicken spice and flour. Divide the flour mixture in half and place the second half in another medium bowl along with with the bits, the rosemary, and the basil.

MAKE THE WET BATTER
In a small bowl, combine the soy milk and vinegar and let it curdle for 5 minutes. Stir in the yogurt, Sriracha, and lemon zest, combining thoroughly. The consistency should be creamy and egg-like. If it's too thick, add a little more soy milk; if it's too thin, add more yogurt.

COAT THE NUGGETS
1. Before you start breading and frying, set up your work area. See Get Set Up on page 33 for instructions.

THE MEAT-IFICATION OF TOFU

My "Warning" nuggets have been a source of controversy and passion ever since I first made them. Many people are now seriously addicted to them. Despite all the fuss, we'd never seen a reaction from a big meat-eater (and non-tofu-eater), so one time we did an experiment. Our subject was my friend's father, who's well into his fifties and not interested in tofu whatsoever. He resisted at first, but we pleaded with him and he finally caved. After one taste he said the funniest shit ever: "You humanized tofu!" This dish really resonates, even with the carnivores among us.

In another nugget "incident," a very angry, straight-edge vegan punk dude took a bite of one and basically spat it back at me. I took the high road and explained to him that I did *not* feed him chicken. I had to convince him that the tofu I use is fermented—that's how I get one-of-a-kind flavor and texture.

Finally, here's how I came up with the name: I was in New York cooking up at a party, and a woman tried a nugget and then looked confused when I told her what it was. "You need a sign that says, 'Warning, Tastes like Chicken!'" she said. And that was that.

2. Working in batches, place several pieces of your chosen protein in the bowl of spiced flour, dredging to coat. Set the coated pieces on a plate. When finished coating, pour any leftover flour into the bits bowl and stir to combine.

3. With one hand, dip each coated piece into the wet batter. With the other (dry) hand, dig a well in the bits mixture and bury the pieces. Gently lift each piece out of the bits and carefully tap off the excess coating.

4. Set the nuggets on a wire rack for 20 minutes before frying to set the crust.

FLAVORING TOFU

If you're using unflavored tofu, marinate overnight in a mixture of 1/4 cup olive oil, 1/4 teaspoon salt, 1/4 teaspoon freshly ground black pepper, and 1/4 teaspoon Chinese Five Spice powder.

FRY THE NUGGETS

1. Meanwhile, prepare your deep fryer according to the instructions or fill a heavy-bottomed, high-sided 12-inch frying pan (preferably cast iron) or 6-quart Dutch oven about one third full with oil. Heat on medium to 315°F.

2. Working in batches, fry these shorties in the hot oil until they are golden brown and floating, about 5 minutes. Tofu cooks in half the time as chicken, so don't sleep on these. Serve them hot with Apricot Crack Sauce (page 202) and vegan Coconut-Honey Biscuits (page 172). Remember with vegan biscuits you have to replace the butter with Earth Balance Buttery Spread and the buttermilk with sour soy milk.

ISLAND

SMOTHERED
♥TOFU♥

I came up with this dish one night when we had our one-year DFC episode anniversary party back in 2008 in Williamsburg, Brooklyn, at what used to be a warehouse called Supreme Trading. It was one of the most fun cook ups we've ever done. The party featured a fashion show curated by design colonist 21MC; live ice sculpting; a bare wall for tagging up art; and a crazy mix of live performers and DJs. It was a frigid January night with 400 hungry-ass people, and I was fashionably late with the food. When I went to plug in my deep fryers, *BOOM!* The sound system went out, and I had to think quickly. I rushed over to a friend's loft and concocted this recipe from food I grew up with. Man, people went bananas. It was like the UN dropping off food-relief aid! These nuggets are perfect served over your favorite grain with a pile of steamed veggies on the side.

SERVES **6**   PREP AND COOKING TIME **1 hour**

CHOOSE 1 PROTEIN:
2 lbs. tofu nuggets, flavored or unflavored (see page 49)
2 lbs. mock meat
2 lbs. mock meat (see pages 198–199 for my seitan and tempeh recipes), cut into nuggets

DRY COATING
¾ cup all-purpose flour
A pinch of garlic powder
A pinch of paprika

2 tsps. sea salt
A pinch of freshly ground black pepper

GRAVY
½ cup Earth Balance Natural Buttery Spread
1 onion, chopped
3 celery stalks, chopped
6 medium carrots, chopped
1 red bell pepper, ribs and seeds removed, chopped

3 garlic cloves, chopped
2 tbsps. all-purpose flour
2 cups coconut water broth (see Note)
1 13.66-oz. can coconut milk
1 tsp. Amino acids, preferably Bragg's, to taste
¼ tsp. cayenne pepper, to taste
½ cup golden raisins
½ cup toasted coconut flakes

COCONUT BROTH

To make coconut water broth, add two teaspoons of veggie bouillon to coconut water.

COAT THE NUGGETS
In a medium bowl, combine the flour, garlic powder, paprika, salt, and pepper. Dredge each tofu piece in the flour mixture and place the coated pieces on a plate.

MAY WAH

I get my tofu from May Wah, a really cool company in New York City known for its amazing array of vegetable proteins. I consider them the best in the business and have been buying from them for ten years. Their black pepper "beef," made from mushrooms, is insane, and I swear by their fermented tofu. If you don't live in NYC, check out one of their distribution outlets throughout the United States, or order their products online—they'll ship them right to you.

SAUTÉ THE NUGGETS

In 12-inch skillet set on medium-high, melt the Earth Balance. Working in batches, brown the tofu pieces on all sides, about 5 to 6 minutes per batch. Return them to the plate.

MAKE THE GRAVY

1. Reduce the heat to medium-low and stir in the onion, celery, carrots, bell pepper, and garlic. Sauté until tender, about 5 minutes. Sprinkle in the flour, stir, and cook 5 minutes more. Pour in the coconut water broth and coconut milk, stirring to combine. Season with amino acids and cayenne pepper. Bring to a boil, and then reduce heat to low.

2. Return the browned tofu pieces to the skillet and add the raisins. Cover and continue cooking until the gravy has thickened, about 30 minutes. If the gravy is too thick, add more coconut water.

3. Serve over your favorite grain; top with the toasted coconut flakes.

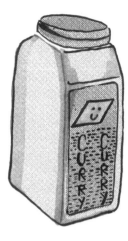

JUST FRY IT !

DANTE FRIED
CHICKEN

THEOPHILUS
LONDON

MELO X

THE BLESSINGS

RUSTIE

KFC RIP

WE COOK UP!

CHAPTER 2

MAIN COURSES

KEEPIN IT REAL IN THE KITCH

When I was a kid, all I wanted to do was draw comic books. Every summer from as far back as I can remember until I was 13 years old, I would sit at my grandmother's kitchen table in Los Angeles drawing comics while helping her hand-churn ice cream in a battered wooden ice cream maker. I was her little guy who would get toys in exchange for taking part in the prep work.

Grans' kitchen was where my love of food was born—it was the beginning of my celebrations with food. I come from a very broken and dysfunctional family, but there was one thing that kept us together. It was food—food in the form of epic dishes cooked up at special family events and parties when no one would fight or argue.

I return to food from my background because I believe that love and energy are transferrable via food. If the love you have for your family goes into your dishes, I think everyone can taste it. Just like music, there's a primal energy from our ancestors that can be passed on.

JEAN'S SL⊙W-SCHOOL CHILI (YOU CAN WAIT!)

This is a memorable dish from growing up because my grans added a really hot and spicy kick; I remember my little cousins and me acclimating to the heat of this chili by turning it into a game. We'd be sucking on ice cubes, taking bites of chili, and betting who could take the most heat—even the toddlers joined in. My family likes spicy food, so we were feelin' this one. One of the great things about this dish is that it feeds an entire family from one pot and is also freezer-friendly. Chili is the ol' American mainstay, and our recipe pretty much keeps with the age-old traditions.

SERVES **4 as an entrée or 8 as an appetizer**   PREP AND COOKING TIME **1 ½ to 4 hours**

- 3 lbs. stew meat (beef, pork, and/or lamb) cut into ½-in. cubes
- 2 tbsps. peanut oil
- 1½ tsps. sea salt
- 1 lb. ground turkey
- 1 small yellow onion, chopped
- 3 garlic cloves, minced
- 1 12-oz. can light-colored beer
- 1 lb. dried pinto beans, rinsed and picked over

- 1 14-oz. can diced tomatoes, with juices
- ½ red bell pepper, ribs and seeds removed, diced
- 2 chipotle peppers, *en adobo*, chopped
- 1 tbsp. adobo sauce
- 1 tbsp. tomato paste
- ¼ cup light brown sugar, packed
- 1 tbsp. chili powder

- 1 tsp. ground cumin
- 2 tsps. cayenne pepper
- ¼ tsp. dried mixed Italian herbs
- 2 cups water, plus more if needed
- 4 cups Veggie Stock (page 154)
- 1 smoked ham hock
  Vegetable oil for sautéing

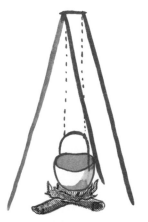

1. In a large bowl, toss the stew meat with the peanut oil and the salt. Set aside.
2. Heat a 6-quart Dutch oven or heavy-bottomed pot on high until hot, about 5 minutes. Working in batches, brown the stew meat on all sides, about 2 minutes per batch. Transfer the browned meat to a large, clean bowl. Lower the heat to medium.
3. Add the ground turkey to the pot and, with a wooden spoon or spatula, break up the turkey as it browns, about 5 minutes. Transfer it to the bowl with the stew meat. Keep the Dutch oven on medium.

MY GREAT-GRANDMOTHER, MINNIE HALL

A significant part of my culinary influence can be traced back to the amazing Minnie Hall, my great-grandmother on my mom's side. She lived to be 101! A socialite, Minnie owned several BBQ restaurants and was the first African-American woman in St. Louis to open up a high-society club, in the 1920s. She was known for her slamming BBQ sauce and her legendary fried pies.

MY GRANDMOTHER, JEAN CRAWFORD

Jean Crawford. I love her to death, but what a complex lady. A strong, caring, God-fearing, and family-oriented woman, she is responsible for the bulk of my culinary aspirations. I grew up in her kitchen every summer, churning butter, making ice cream, cleaning out the chitterlings . . . which, by the way, was pretty gross. She was a real grandmother from back-in-the-day *and* a real foodie. She made her own BBQ pits and kept backyard freezers with locks on them. Firmly old school, she was against eating anything synthetic like chips or Oreos, which she called *fake food*. Jean would rather bake off her own cookies. That's probably why I have such a strong view on not eating industrialized and processed food; I saw my grandmother go to war with it in the 1980s.

Originally from Louisiana, she moved from New Orleans to Los Angeles in the 1960s, bringing Creole cooking, the culinary melting pot of America, along with her. With its Caribbean, African, Indigenous Indian, and European influences, Creole cooking was inspired by other cultures, as are the people who make it. Jean was no different. She would invite Mexican, Korean, and Chinese friends in LA into her home, and they would all share recipes and techniques. Jean had a genius for sampling ingredients and flavors; she blended tastes and textures from different cultures and used them to enhance her own creations. As a woman living in the 'hood, that was pretty avant-garde for the time. Her sauerkraut took notes from kimchi, and she made the most bad-ass stir-fry I've ever tasted. She was also a well-respected caterer. I remember going with her when she cooked up for Lucille Ball, Rita Hayworth, and Charlton Heston—all these crazy Hollywood stars from the golden age.

Looking back, it's clear how much my grandmother's craft shaped my own. I thank her for the knowledge and love she passed on to me.

4. Add the onion and garlic and sauté for about 3 minutes, then pour the beer into the pot to deglaze it, five minutes more.
5. Add the beans, canned tomatoes, bell pepper, chipotle peppers, adobo sauce, tomato paste, brown sugar, chili powder, cumin, cayenne, and mixed herbs, and simmer until fragrant, about 4 minutes.
6. Add the water, stock, ham hock, stew meat, and browned turkey to pot, and bring to a boil. Reduce heat to medium-low and simmer, with the lid slightly askew, for 1½ hours. Check the chili occasionally and give it a stir. For a really rich gravy, simmer for 2 to 3 hours. Garnish the chili with crushed crackers, avocado, pico de gallo, and sour cream. Serve it with some cornbread or just eat it naked.

MY GRANDFATHER, JIMMY FORREST

My food is all about heritage, and one important part of my heritage is my grandfather, Jimmy Forrest, who was an acclaimed jazz musician. In 1952, Jimmy wrote the Billboard R&B number-one song "Night Train," which was covered a decade later by Mr. James Brown. It was sampled by Public Enemy too! My granddad also played with Miles Davis, Duke Ellington, and Count Basie's Orchestra as a tenor saxophonist. As long as I can remember, our family was immersed in music. When we were young, we'd be chilling with my granddad while he had all these grown folk over. I didn't know at the time that one of them was Miles Davis!

JEAN'S COOK-UP GUMBO

I remember being bounced around by my grandmother as a wee lad, cushioned in her large bosom as she stood over the big-ass kettle-pot contraption in the backyard and cooked up gumbo. OK, truth? I don't actually remember that. She did it with my younger siblings, though, so I'm assuming I got the same treatment. Like all her dishes, Grans' gumbo had tons of different cultural influences, as do all other gumbos—this mix of cultures is what, to me, makes it the most quintessential American dish. I've had many different variations depending on season, available ingredients, region—you get the point. Don't be intimidated by the many steps in this recipe—just be patient and know that you will land on your feet. Serve this one-pot dish with grains.

SERVES **8 to 10**   PREP AND COOKING TIME **2 ½ hours**

- 1 large poblano pepper, fire roasted, ribs and seeds removed, chopped
- 6 cups Gumbo Stock (see Note on page 60 and recipe on page 195)
- 1 lb. skinless, boneless chicken breasts, cut into bite-size pieces
- 1 lb. Andouille or lean smoked sausage, cut into bite-size pieces
- ½ cup peanut oil, canola oil, or bacon drippings

- ¾ cup all-purpose flour
- 3 medium onions, chopped
- 6 celery stalks, chopped
- 2 red bell peppers, ribs and seeds removed, chopped
- 4 tbsps. minced garlic
- 1 cup cherry tomatoes, whole
- 1 tsp. Old Bay or DFC Fish Fry Spice Mix (page 189)
- 1 tsp. fresh thyme leaves, chopped
- ½ tsp. red pepper flakes
- 2 dried bay leaves
  A squirt of amino acids, preferably Bragg's

- 1 tsp. Sriracha
- 1 lb. medium shrimp, peeled, tails removed
- 6 to 8 Alaskan crab legs
  Half of a 14-oz. can of baby corn, preferably Native Forest
- ½ lb. okra, chopped and roasted (see Note)
- ½ cup chopped fresh parsley

HOW TO ROAST OKRA

To roast okra, preheat oven to 350°F. In a medium bowl, toss the okra with 1 tablespoon olive oil and season to taste with salt and pepper. Roast for 15 minutes, or until slightly crispy. Let cool, then chop the okra into 1-inch pieces.

GUMBO IS ALL ABOUT THE STOCK

It cannot be a good gumbo without homemade stock. Even though I get down with bouillon broths, keep it real when you make the gumbo. Try making the stock a day before you make the gumbo. It takes a couple hours, but it's so worth it.

1. In a blender, purée the poblano with 2 cups of the gumbo stock. Add the purée to the remaining 4 cups of gumbo stock.
2. In a large, heavy-bottomed pot set on medium-high and coated with 1 tablespoon oil, sauté the chicken and sausage in batches until browned on all sides, about 5 to 8 minutes. Some meat sticking to the bottom of the pot is a good thing, trust me. Transfer the sautéed chicken and sausage to medium bowl. Set aside.
3. Pour the remaining oil and all of the flour in pot, stirring constantly until a roux forms, about 20 minutes. The roux is ready when it's the color of red brick or milk chocolate.
4. Add the onions, celery, bell peppers, and garlic, and cook on low heat for 8 to 10 minutes.
5. Gradually add the gumbo stock to the pot, stirring constantly until blended. If you add the stock too quickly, clumps may form.
6. Add the chicken and sausage, tomatoes, Old Bay or DFC Fish Fry Spice Mix, thyme, red pepper, bay leaves, amino acids, and Sriracha. Cover the pot and simmer on low heat for 30 minutes. Remove the lid and cook 30 more minutes, stirring occasionally.
7. Add the shrimp, crab legs, corn, okra, and parsley, and continue to cook on low heat, uncovered, for 15 minutes. I like to serve the gumbo in big-old coffee mugs over rice and a side of potato salad, for the Low Country effect, or with mixed greens and French bread.

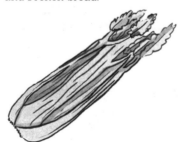

JON-JON'S SUNDAY ROAST

I loved Sundays when I was a kid. There would always be a roast in the oven, and if we were lucky we'd get the ginger-beef version with Filipino spices in it. I adapted the recipe to include jicama and plantains. I know this dish is a little involved, but honestly, once you get past studding the meat, it's downright easy. This recipe will feed six people very well or eight if served with sides—we always ate it with cornbread and collard greens. I like to pour the gravy over each individual serving of meat and roasted veggies. This dish is rustic in appearance, so don't be looking for any pretty pot roast here.

SERVES **6 to 8**   PREP AND COOKING TIME **4 ½ hours**

- 3 sprigs rosemary, stems discarded, leaves minced
- 12 garlic cloves, 10 minced and 2 cut into slivers
- 3 thumb-size pieces of fresh, peeled ginger, 2 grated and 1 cut into slivers
- 5 to 6 lbs. boneless chuck roast
- ½ cup all-purpose flour
- 1 tsp. sea salt
- 1 tsp. freshly ground black pepper, plus more to taste
- 1 tsp. paprika

- 1 tsp. onion powder
- 1 tsp. garlic powder
- 1 tbsp. bacon fat or canola oil
- 1 tbsp. olive oil
- 1 tbsp. butter
- 2 cups Beef Stock (page 196), warm
- 1 cup Guinness stout
- 1 tbsp. light brown sugar
- 1 tbsp. toasted sesame oil
- 1 cup dried onions
- 1 tbsp. amino acids, preferably Bragg's

- 1 large bay leaf
- 1 tsp. mixed dried Italian herbs
- 2 ripe plantains, peeled and cut into 3-in.-thick pieces
- 1 8-oz. can of water chestnuts
- 4 turnips, peeled and cut into large chunks
- 3 large sweet potatoes, peeled and cut into large chunks
- 1 large sweet onion, quartered
- 2 to 3 green tomatoes, quartered
- 2 celery stalks, coarsely chopped

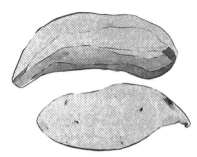

PREP THE ROAST

1. Preheat oven to 350°F.
2. In a small mixing bowl, combine the rosemary, minced garlic, and grated ginger. Set aside.
3. Stud the roast by using the tip of a paring knife to cut multiple small, deep slits (1½ to 2 inches each) all over the meat (make at least 25 slits). While making the slits, push back the meat to expose the opening and press ⅛ tsp. of the rosemary mixture into each slit, packing it tight with your finger.
4. In a small bowl, combine ¼ cup flour, salt, pepper, paprika, onion powder, and garlic powder.

5. Pour half of the flour mixture onto a shallow plate and place meat on top. Sprinkle remaining flour mix over the top of roast and rub it into meat, turning until covered on all the sides. Let rest for 15 minutes.

6. In an 8-quart Dutch oven set on medium-high, heat the bacon fat or canola oil. Using two large tongs or two large forks, carefully place the roast into the hot fat and sear it on all sides until very brown, about 3 to 5 minutes per side. Remove roast from pot and set aside on a plate. If there are charred bits in the pan, add a tablespoon of water and break up the meat bits with a wooden spoon. Stir until water evaporates.

MAKE THE GRAVY BASE

1. Add the olive oil and butter to the Dutch oven. Sprinkle the remaining flour and cook, stirring constantly, until mixture becomes the color of peanut butter, about 5 to 7 minutes.

2. Stir in the warm beef broth, Guinness, brown sugar, sesame oil, dried onions, ginger and garlic slivers, amino acids, bay leaf, and mixed herbs.

ROAST THE BEEF

1. Place roast on top of the mixture and spoon some liquid over the roast. Cover with a lid or foil and bake, basting occasionally, for 2½ to 3 hours, or until very tender.

2. Remove roast from oven, baste the meat, and arrange the plantains, chestnuts, turnips, sweet potatoes, and onion around the sides of the roast.

3. Cover and return to oven for 1 hour more, basting the veggies occasionally. Add the green tomatoes and celery and continue roasting for 20 minutes, or until veggies are done. Carefully transfer the roast and vegetables to a serving dish.

FINISH THE GRAVY

Skim off any visible fat from the liquid in Dutch oven. Bring gravy to boil on top of the stove. Reduce heat and simmer until gravy is thickened enough to coat the back of a spoon, and serve alongside the roast and veggies.

DO OR DIE
BED-STUY
SHEPHERD'S PIE

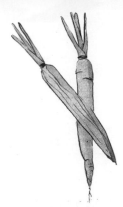

Growin' up, we ate shepherd's pie once a week in winter months; it just resonated with family love energy. I like the sweet taste of the leeks in the mashed yams in this primal meal, and then there are the chanterelle mushrooms (yum!). One fall in my Bed-Stuy loft in Brooklyn, I'd just come back from Sweden where I'd been introduced to chanterelles; I decided to make my family's gravy with them. I also roasted the veggies beforehand instead of boiling them, the traditional way, and then scattered crispy, deep-fried leeks over the top. So now you feel me? Shepherd's Pie is a British institution, but when I served this dish in London, people actually cried. No joke. And they thought we Yankees couldn't get down with the Shep Pie game...

SERVES **5 to 8**   PREP AND COOKING TIME **1 ½ hours**

VEGGIE LAYER

- 1 lb. broccoli, stems removed, florets coarsely chopped
- 2 small beets (red or golden), peeled and diced
- 8 Brussels sprouts, ends removed, quartered
- 1 carrot, diced
- 1 garlic clove, finely chopped
- ½ cup frozen peas, thawed
- 1 turnip, peeled and diced
- ½ cauliflower head, cored and diced into 1-inch pieces
- 3 tbsps. olive oil

POTATO LAYER

- 4 medium Yukon Gold potatoes, peeled and quartered
- 2 large sweet potatoes, peeled and quartered
- 4 tbsps. unsalted butter

- ½ cup heavy cream
  Sea salt and freshly ground black pepper

GRAVY

- 3 tbsps. unsalted butter
- 1 shallot, diced
- 1 lb. chanterelle mushrooms, wiped clean and finely chopped; if not in season, substitute shiitake or oyster mushrooms
- ¼ cup Self-Rising Flour (page 192)
- 2 ½ cups Beef Stock (page 196), or whatever stock you have on hand
- ½ cup heavy cream
  Sea salt and ground white pepper

MEAT LAYER

- 2 tbsps. olive oil
- ½ medium yellow onion, diced
- 1 red bell pepper, ribs and seeds removed, diced

- 1 lb. ground beef
- 1 lb. ground lamb
  Freshly ground black pepper
- 1 tsp. sea salt
- 3 tbsps. chili powder
- 1 garlic clove, chopped
- 3 tbsps. tomato paste (optional)
- 3 tbsps. tequila

TOPPING

- 1½ to 2 cups grated mild Cheddar cheese
- 1 cup grated Parmesan
- 5 leeks, sliced in half, the white and light green parts julienned and washed
  Peanut oil

SPECIAL EQUIPMENT

Hand mixer or immersion blender
Candy thermometer

~~~~~~

MAKE THE VEGGIE LAYER

1. Preheat oven to 425°F.

2. In a large bowl, toss all the veggie layer ingredients together with the olive oil. Arrange the coated veggies in a single layer on a baking sheet and roast 20 to 25 minutes, until slightly crispy. Remove from oven, set aside, and decrease oven temperature to 350°F.

MAKE THE POTATO LAYER

1. Bring to boil a stock pot filled a little more than halfway with salted water. Add the potatoes and cook, uncovered, until tender, about 15 minutes. Drain and return the potatoes to the pot.

2. With a potato masher, mix the butter and cream into the potatoes. With an immersion blender or electric hand mixer on medium speed, whip the potatoes until smooth, about 3 minutes. A heavy-duty whisk or a fork will work too. If using one of those, have at it for 5 minutes. Add salt and pepper to taste.

MAKE THE GRAVY

1. In a 2½-quart sauce pan over medium heat, melt butter, swirling to coat the pan. Add the shallot and garlic, and sauté until soft but not browned, about 1 minute. Add the mushrooms and sauté, stirring frequently, until they soften and give up their juices, about 5 minutes.

2. Meanwhile, in a small bowl or measuring cup, whisk together the flour and ½ cup of the stock until the flour is incorporated. Add remaining 2 cups stock to the mushrooms in the pan and bring to a boil. Reduce heat to low.

3. Slowly whisk in the flour mixture and the cream, and simmer until the gravy thickens, about 5 minutes. Taste and adjust the seasoning with salt and pepper. Keep gravy warm.

MAKE THE MEAT LAYER

1. In a 12-inch skillet set on medium-high, heat the olive oil until shimmering. Sauté the onions and peppers until translucent, about 3 minutes. Add meats and cook until browned, about 5 to 7 minutes.

2. Add all of the spices and season with salt and pepper. Let them work together for a few minutes, then add the tomato paste, if using. Pour in the tequila, and cook on low for about 10 minutes. Remove from heat.

(PAN SIZE)

The 12-inch pan gives you enough room to render the water from the meat without steaming it. Don't steam your meat!

KEEP IT NEAT

Presentation is key, so keep this in mind when you put the casserole together—don't slop on the layers.

LAYER THE CASSEROLE

1. Using a paper towel or pastry brush, lightly coat a 9 x 13-inch casserole dish with olive oil. Press the cooked meat firmly into the bottom of the casserole dish with a spoon or spatula (see Note).

2. In a mixing bowl, combine the roasted veggies with 1 to 2 cups gravy, depending on how saucy you like it. Then very lightly spread the veggie-gravy mixture on top of the meat.

3. Evenly spread the potatoes over the meat and veg. Sprinkle the cheeses on top.

BAKE UP AND MAKE THE TOPPING

1. Bake, uncovered, 30 to 45 minutes; the cheese will be browned. Not brown enough for ya? Put it under the boiler for 1 to 2 minutes to brown at the very end. Remove the Do or Die from the oven and let it sit while you make the crispy leeks.

2. Add 1 inch of peanut oil to a small, heavy sauce pan and heat to 350°F.

3. In small batches, fry the leeks until golden brown, about 30 to 60 seconds per batch. Remove them from the oil with a slotted spoon and place them on paper towels to drain.

4. Evenly distribute the crispy leeks over top of the Do or Die. Use any leftover gravy to garnish the bottoms of the serving plates.

YAM-BANANA CATFISH

I promise this is unlike any other catfish dish you've ever had. This recipe has some borderline magical properties; years ago, it had the power to quiet down any feud at my house in a matter of moments. Its secret weapon is the well-seasoned crust, made with cornmeal, lil' crunchy yam fries, and the subtly sweet banana. This dish is well complemented by a side of DFC Succotash (page 130). Oh, and one more thing: I hereby dedicate Yam-Banana Catfish to my cousin Promise Smith, who loves it and calls it Catfish Scampi. *POW!*

SERVES **4**   PREP AND COOKING TIME **1 hour**

8 4-oz. farm-raised catfish fillets
  A few pinches of salt
1 large lemon, juiced

CATFISH COATING

2 large yams, peeled
  and shredded
4 scallions, white and green
  parts thinly sliced
1 cup crushed banana chips
2 cups yellow cornmeal

1 cup all-purpose flour
2 tsps. cayenne pepper
2 tsps. paprika
2 to 4 tsps. Old Bay seasoning
2 tsps. ground cumin
  A pinch of nutmeg,
  preferably freshly grated
  A pinch of cinnamon
1 tbsp. black peppercorns,
  crushed
1 tsp. onion powder

WET BATTER

1 tbsp. plain yogurt or buttermilk
1 large egg
½ cup water
1 gallon canola oil

SPECIAL EQUIPMENT

Candy thermometer

A lot of people don't care for catfish, but I love its texture. When I first tried blackened catfish as a kid, I loved the sweet, smoky, buttery flavor. It's meaty and flaky and holds up to strong flavors. And versatile, too— you can use it for everything from a fish fry to a stew. Catfish gets a bad rap for tasting overly fishy, but there's a simple technique that a lot of Southern and Caribbean cultures use to clean their fish: soak it in ice water with salt and lemon. The bias against catfish is slipping away, though. The last time I was in the UK I noticed that with haddock and cod stocks dwindling, the Brits have turned to catfish as a sustainable alternative for their traditional fish and chips!

~~~~~

COAT THE CATFISH

1. Before you start breading and frying, set up your work area. See Get Set Up (page 33) for instructions.
2. In a medium bowl, combine the shredded yams, sliced scallions, and crushed banana chips.
3. In a shallow plate (I use a pie plate) stir together the remaining coating ingredients.
4. In a large bowl, combine the buttermilk, egg, and some water (about ½ cup).
5. Using one hand, dredge catfish strips in flour mixture, then, with your other hand, dip fish into buttermilk mixture. Let batter drip off before moving on to yam mixture.
6. Using your dry hand, coat the battered strips in the yam mixture. Let set on a wire rack for 20 minutes.

FRY THE CATFISH

1. Meanwhile, prepare a deep fryer according to the instructions or fill a heavy, 12-inch skillet (preferably cast iron) a third of the way with the oil, and heat it on medium to 325°F. Use a candy thermometer to check the oil temperature.
2. Working in batches, add a few catfish strips to the hot oil. Fry for 5 to 7 minutes, flipping halfway through, or until golden brown. Carefully remove the fried fish from the oil and place on the draining station. Serve with DFC Boujee Ranch Sauce (page 200) or your favorite tartar sauce.

THE INFAMOUS DFC ROOFTOP PARTY

One of my all-time favorite DFC parties was the fish fry rooftop blowout in Bushwick, Brooklyn, with performances by Spank Rock, Mapai, The Carps, and KUDU. It was the first time I introduced Yam-Banana Catfish to a crowd, and it was pretty hot. The cops showed up, and I thought they were going tear it down (we had Yo Majesty!, shirtless, dissing the officers). But the cops were cool and let us continue. It was a really stressful day for me, lugging the sound system, ice sculptures, and all of the cooking equipment up to the roof. But it was one of those perfect days—that party was talked about for two years straight. It put us on the map.

BANANA-DATE ~~SHORT~~ ♥RIBS♥

LA has the most incredible Korean BBQ spots—growing up, I thought they were so exotic.
I also thought it was cool that my grandmother ate these foods. She had a trade system
going with some spots, swapping fried chicken, mac and cheese, and dinner rolls for Korean
BBQ beef ribs from her neighbors. She went absolutely ham over those. For this recipe
I went ahead and laced the ribs with ingredients I remember from the dishes we ate on my
first excursions into unfamiliar LA territory. They will always hold a special place in
my culinary soul.

SERVES **10**   PREP AND COOKING TIME **7 hours, plus 6 hours to overnight marinating**

RIBS

10 lbs. short ribs, silver skin
   removed (see Note) and
   sliced into individual ribs
   Olive oil
1 to 2 cups DFC Meat Rub
   (page 191), or your favorite
   seasoned salt mixed with
   chili powder in a 1:4 ratio

SAUCE

1 tbsp. paprika, sweet
   or smoked
2 tsps. black pepper
1 tbsp. chili powder
2 tsps. ground cumin
1 tbsp. unsalted butter
   or bacon fat
2 tsps. sesame oil
1 medium onion, finely chopped
4 cloves garlic, minced
1 thumb-size piece of fresh
   ginger, peeled and minced
1 red bell pepper, ribs and
   seeds removed, chopped
1 tomato, chopped

1 cup dark sesame seeds,
   toasted and crushed
2 bananas, sliced into ¼-inch-
   thick pieces
3 cups dates, pitted
1 cup beer (any lager will do)
2 cups stock (beef or whatever
   you have on hand)
¼ cup apple cider vinegar,
   preferably Bragg's
3 tbsps. amino acids,
   preferably Bragg's,
   or light soy sauce
¼ cup tomato paste
3 tbsps. molasses
2 tsps. Sriracha

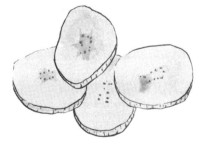

SPICE THE RIBS

1. In a large bowl or shallow dish, lightly coat the ribs with oil.
2. Thoroughly coat ribs with DFC meat rub, cover in plastic film,
and refrigerate for at least 6 hours or overnight.

WOOD CHOICE

I like pecan or
mesquite for beef.

RIB PREP

If the butcher hasn't
already taken care of it,
trim the fat and remove
the tough silver skin
from the top of the
ribs. The silver skin is
the membrane that
is attached to the back
of the rib bones; it will
prevent the smoke and
any rub flavorings from
penetrating the meat.
It needs to go! Just peel
it off with a knife at the
corner, and then use
your fingers to rip the
whole thing off.

SMOKE THE RIBS

1. Remove the ribs from the fridge and set up your BBQ pit or grill for smoking (page 24) and preheat to 225°F.
2. Put marinated ribs into the BBQ, bone side down on the indirect heat side of the grill, and add the wood. Too much smoke will ruin the meat, so add no more than 2 to 4 ounces to a tight-lidded smoker. Keep the lid on, and resist peeking until about three-quarters of the way through the cooking time.
3. If your ribs are about 1 inch thick, smoke them for about 3 hours, or until the internal temperature of the meat reaches 180°F. If the ribs are 1½ inches thick, they'll hit 180°F in about 3½ hours. You lucky ones with ribs 2 inches thick will have to wait about 4 hours until the ribs are 180°F. When meat is done, take it out of the pit and let it rest for 10 minutes on a serving platter.

MAKE THE SAUCE

1. While the ribs are cooking, in a small bowl, combine the paprika, black pepper, chili powder, and cumin, and set aside.
2. In a medium sauté pan set on medium, melt the butter or bacon fat and sesame oil. Add the onion and cook until translucent, about 5 minutes.
3. Add the garlic, ginger, bell pepper, tomato, sesame seeds, bananas, and dates. Stir in the spice mix. Cook for 3 minutes.
4. Transfer the mixture to a blender, add remaining sauce ingredients, and purée. Once the sauce is smooth, pour it into a 4-quart sauce pan and simmer on low for 15 minutes. The consistency should be like a thin steak sauce. Add more beer, water, or stock if the consistency is too thick. Keep warm.
5. Bathe the ribs with the warm sauce, and serve. Extra sauce will keep in the fridge in an airtight container for a week.

MOFONGO TAMALES

Tamales are a huge part of my heritage and also the culinary embodiment of Mexican culture (though there are just as many versions of tamales as Latin American regions). I remember my grandmother in the kitchen with all sorts of Mexican women who taught her how to make tamales, tortillas, tripe, refried beans, and chile rellenos. This was a cultural education right before my eyes. I updated her tamales by adding mashed plantains into the dough. Tamales are very time consuming and difficult to master so keep with it—patience and mad practice are the key to success.

SERVES **24 to 30 (yields 4 to 5 dozen; estimate 2 tamales per person)**   PREP AND COOKING TIME **48 hours**

GUMBO
- 1 recipe Chicken Stock (page 195), about 10 cups
- 2 tbsps. canola oil
- 4 Andouille sausages (chicken or pork), diced
- ¼ cup beer (lager is good here)
- 4 tbsps. unsalted butter
- 4 tbsps. all-purpose flour
- 4 cups shredded chicken picked from the stock carcasses
- 1 medium sweet onion, diced
- 2 celery stalks, diced
- 1 red bell pepper, ribs and seeds removed, diced
- 2 garlic cloves, minced
- 2 tbsps. Old Bay seasoning, crab boil, or DFC Fish Fry Spice Mix (page 192)
- 10 okra (roasted if you like, see Note), cut into 1-in. pieces (optional)
- 1 lb. boneless salmon fillet, cut into 1-in. pieces
- Sea salt and freshly ground pepper

TAMALE
- 2 packs corn husks
- 4 large, ripe sweet plantains, peeled
- 4 tbsps. unsalted butter
- 2½ cups lard, vegetable shortening, or duck fat
- 4 tsps. sea salt
- 3 tbsps. ground cumin, toasted (see Note)
- 1 tsp. chili powder, or to taste
- 1 tsp. white pepper

TRY THIS

Toast cumin in a small sauté pan until fragrant, about 2 or 3 minutes over medium heat.

DAY 1: GUMBO PREP

1. Make the stock. Reserve the vegetables, and remember to pick the chicken meat off the bones and set it aside (you'll be adding it to the gumbo).

2. Put the reserved vegetables into a blender. Add some stock, and process until smooth. Stir the purée into the stock. Season the stock with salt and pepper to taste.

3. In a 6-quart Dutch oven or heavy-bottomed stock pot set on medium, heat 1 tablespoon oil. Fry the sausage until crispy brown, remove from pan. Pour in the beer to deglaze pot, working up the brown bits with a wooden spoon. Add the butter and flour and stir continuously to make a roux, until a blond caramel color develops, about 7 minutes. Don't walk away. The roux will burn if left unattended. Add more butter if flour is too dry or clumpy.

HOW TO ROAST OKRA

To roast okra, preheat oven to 350°F. In a medium bowl, toss the okra with 1 tablespoon olive oil and season to taste with salt and pepper. Roast for 15 minutes, or until slightly crispy. Let cool, then chop the okra into 1-inch pieces.

FREEZE TAMALES

You can freeze tamales up to 2 years if vacuumed sealed, or 6 months in an airtight container. I don't recommend freezing seafood tamales in a container—you should vacuum-seal them.

FILL IT

Fill your tamales with anything you can imagine. I've done smoked Gouda cheese, roasted chicken, beef stew, and roasted asparagus. Just do you!

4. Add the sausage and shredded chicken to the roux, and slowly add enough stock to cover, stirring constantly. Save remaining stock for the masa dough.

5. In a small sauté pan set on medium, add the onion, celery, and bell pepper. Sauté until translucent, about 5 minutes. Add the garlic, sauté another 2 minutes. Stir in the Old Bay, or spice of your choice.

6. Add sautéed onion, celery, and garlic to the sausage mixture and simmer for 1 hour.

7. During the final minutes of cooking the gumbo, add the salmon and continue to simmer. The salmon will be falling apart when it's done, about 3 to 4 minutes.

8. Remove gumbo from heat and cool completely. Cover and refrigerate overnight.

9. Place the corn husks in a large, clean, food-safe vessel and cover with warm water. You may have to put a plate on top of the husks to weigh them down. It's important they stay submerged, or the husks will dry out. Soak overnight in a warm spot.

DAY 2: TAMALE TIME

1. Remove husks from water and pat dry. Place them in a covered dish or large plastic bag to prevent them from drying out. Use only the large and medium-size husks for the tamales. The smaller ones can be used later for ties or patches.

2. Cut or tear 6-inch lengths off of some of the smaller or unusable husks to create tie strips. You will tie these around the middle of the tamales to hold the flaps down.

3. In a 4-quart sauce pan, boil the plantains for 8 minutes. Drain and mash plantains with the butter. Set aside.

4. To make the masa, whisk the lard, vegetable shortening, or duck fat until very fluffy. Add mashed plantains, the salt, cumin, and enough chili powder to turn the mixture pink. Add the remaining stock, a little at a time, mixing it with your hands to get a smooth, spreadable consistency, almost like peanut butter. If you run out of stock before the texture is right, use hot water.

5. Using your fingers, spread an $1/8$-inch-thick coating of masa on each corn husk, leaving a ½-inch border along the sides and a 2-inch border along the top and bottom of husks.

6. Drop 2 tablespoons gumbo meat onto the masa.

7. Fold sides of the husks until they just overlap, and then fold the narrow end under. Tie each tamale with prepared strips and place, folded side down, on a baking sheet. Continue filling and folding until you've used all the husks.

8. Fill bottom of a large tamale steamer with a small amount of water, and place the tamales upright in the steamer. Alternatively, use very large stock pot with a colander set in it, keeping the tamales from touching the water. If your steamer doesn't have a lid or if the tamales are bursting over the top, cover the steamer with a damp cloth or leftover tamale husks.

9. Steam tamales until masa is no longer sticky, 60 to 90 minutes.

ROSEMARY-BLACK BEAN ~~CHICKEN~~ -N-DUMPLINGS

This was one of my dad's favorite dishes, which is probably why I refused to eat it as a kid. Looking back, I completely regret missing out on all those dumplings, but I make up for it now. When I first tried chicken and dumplings outside of my family, I was shocked at how different other versions of this popular Southern meal were from ours. No beans? No herbs in the dumplings? No green chilies and ginger broth? No Andouille sausage? It was an education for sure. I urge you to make this version for yourself—you won't be sorry!

SERVES **6 to 8**   PREP AND COOKING TIME **1 ½ hours**

CHICKEN
5 fresh Anaheim green chilies
1 3-lb. chicken, cut into 8 pieces
    (breasts, legs, thighs, wings)
    Sea salt and freshly ground
    black pepper
½ cup all-purpose flour
2 tbsps. unsalted butter
2 tbsp. olive oil
4 Andouille sausages,
    sliced lengthwise
1 medium onion, finely diced
2 medium carrots, finely diced
2 stalks of celery, finely diced

1 thumb-size piece of ginger,
    peeled and cut into matchsticks
1 garlic clove, minced
2 tsp. veggie bouillon, preferably
    Superior Touch
½ tsp. dried mixed Italian herbs
¼ tsp. turmeric
6 cups Chicken or Veggie Stock
    (pages 194–195)
2 tbsp. apple cider vinegar,
    preferably Bragg's
2 cups cooked black beans
½ cup heavy cream

DUMPLINGS
1½ cups all-purpose flour
1 tbsp. white cornmeal
1 tbsp. plus 1 tsp. baking powder
1 tsp. kosher salt
2 tbsps. minced fresh parsley,
    rosemary, or cilantro (optional)
1 tbsp. unsalted butter
4 garlic cloves, minced
1½ cups half and half or heavy cream

MAKE THE CHICKEN
1. Fire roast Anaheim chilies on stove top by holding them over open flames with tongs and blackening the skin. Remove as much of the charred skin as possible and chop chilies into medium pieces. Set aside in a bowl with its juices.
2. Sprinkle chicken pieces with salt and pepper, then dredge both sides in flour.
3. Melt butter with a little olive oil in a medium pot or Dutch oven over medium-high heat. In two batches, brown chicken on both sides and remove to a clean plate. Brown sausage on both sides and chop into little pieces. Set aside on the same plate.

4. In the same pot, add the diced onion, carrots, celery, ginger, and garlic, reduce the heat to medium-low, and cook, stirring frequently, for 3 to 4 minutes. Stir in bouillon, mixed herbs, and turmeric. Add the stock and apple cider vinegar and stir to combine. Stir in browned chicken, sausage, chilies, and beans. Cover pot and simmer for 20 minutes.

5. Remove chicken from pot and set aside on a plate to cool slightly. Using two forks, remove chicken from the bones and then shred the meat. (Careful! It's still kinda hot.) Stir the shredded chicken back into the stock, then pour in the heavy cream, stirring to combine.

MAKE THE DUMPLINGS

1. In a large bowl, sift together all dry ingredients, then stir in the parsley. Set aside.

2. In a small sauce pan set on medium, heat the butter and garlic for 2 minutes. Pour it over the flour mixture. Add the half and half or cream and stir gently until the texture becomes very crumbly. Set aside until you're ready to drop the dough into the stock.

3. Using a large spoon, scoop out a tablespoon or so of dough, then drop it into the stock, repeat until you've added 8 or 10 scoops. Don't fuss with the dumplings, just put the lid on the pot and let it simmer for another 15 minutes. Adjust the seasonings, if needed. Remove the pot from the heat and allow the chicken-n-dumplings to sit for 10 minutes before serving.

ANDOUILLE CORN DOGS

Before the Ride or Fry truck run came to an end, we hit one more out of the ballpark with these corn dogs. I consider them a premium DFC delicacy. Here's how they came to be: we decided to flip the plain ol' corn dog by dipping smoky Andouille sausage in batter laced with chili and Parmesan. The result is completely insane, so brace yourself. It was fun coming up with a dish that has so much DFC personality, yet is inexpensive to make and utterly delicious.

SERVES **8**   PREP AND COOKING TIME **45 minutes**

1 gallon peanut oil
1 cup turkey chili, preferably
  Trader Joe's
½ cup water
1 cup buttermilk
½ cup pale ale
1 tbsp. white sugar (optional)
1 jalapeño pepper, ribs and seeds
  removed, minced (optional)

1 cup yellow cornmeal
1 cup all-purpose flour
2 tsps. sea salt
1 tsp. baking powder
¼ tsp. baking soda
½ tsp. cayenne pepper
1 tsp. chili powder
8 Andouille sausages
1 cup cornstarch

SPECIAL EQUIPMENT
8 wooden skewers or single
  chopsticks
  Candy thermometer

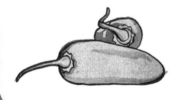

MAKE THE BATTER
1. In a blender or food processor, purée the chili with the water. Transfer to a medium bowl and add the buttermilk, beer, sugar, if using, and jalapeño, if using. Stir to combine.
2. In another medium bowl, combine the cornmeal, flour, salt, baking powder, baking soda, cayenne pepper, and chili powder.
3. Add the chili mixture to the flour mixture, stirring just enough to bring the batter together; there should be lumps. Set aside for 10 minutes.

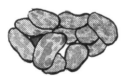

COAT THE SAUSAGES
1. Before you start coating and frying, set up your work area. See Get Set Up (page 33) for instructions.
2. Pierce each sausage with a skewer or chopstick, set aside.
3. Pour the cornstarch into a pie plate or casserole dish. Roll each skewered sausage in cornstarch, tapping it lightly to remove the excess. Set the coated sausages on a wire rack set over newspaper or paper towels.

FRY THOSE DOGS

1. Prepare your deep fryer according to the instructions or fill a high-sided, heavy-bottomed Dutch oven or 12-inch skillet (preferably cast-iron) halfway with oil (about 3 inches) and heat to 375°F (use a candy thermometer to take the oil temperature).
2. Fill two large drinking glasses three-quarters full with the batter.
3. Working 2 at a time, quickly dip a sausage into each glass and immediately and carefully place them into the hot oil. Fry the corn dogs until the coating is golden brown, about 4 to 5 minutes, turning halfway through. Using tongs, remove the sausages one at a time from the oil and place them on the wire rack to drain for 3 to 5 minutes. Repeat until all the sausages are fried. Serve with Hotty Totty Spicy Mustard (page 205).

RIDE OR FRY FOOD TRUCK

I am a chef, but I didn't go to cooking school to learn my trade. Instead, I started off as a dishwasher and worked my way up, apprenticing in kitchens the ol' fashioned way. Cooking in a pop-up gourmet food truck felt like a natural evolution of the constant education I got from working in restaurants. Just like I had to adapt in each new kitchen I worked in, I had to figure out the best ways to work in the truck.

When I first decided to do a truck, it was more viable financially to launch it in Los Angeles than in New York. In April 2010, in order to raise money and press attention for the truck while I was still on the East Coast, my friends and I created an underground fried chicken bike delivery service called Ride or Fry. We took online orders, hit the streets with our bikes, and delivered the food.

After two months of some awesome press from the likes of *New York* magazine as well as an investment meeting with members of a Mormon congregation in Utah, we launched the Ride or Fry truck in LA. We'd only planned to pop up for three months, but by October of that year we'd been crowned winner of Thrillist's citywide Best of the Best Food Truck competition. We ended up running the streets for a year and a half, peddling new DFC street food experiments like the Andouille Corn Dog!

It was an experience, to say the least. In the end it was a big success, but I definitely grappled with some dos and don'ts over those hard-slog eighteen months. Here is some hard-won knowledge for you:

If you are interested in starting a food truck, start off by leasing one from a company like Roadstoves (page 29). Run the streets for three to six months and see how you like it and how the public reacts to your food.

Know your product, and don't do a huge menu. My food is by nature pretty fancy, so I had to tone down my recipes to make them doable in the truck. I learned how to create menus that worked on the street, were economical, and could be cooked up within the confines of the truck. Even so, I always used seasonal ingredients and never served any kind of industrialized meat.

"CANDIED" YAM·N·LAMB ~~STROGANOFF~~

Way back when, my grandmother would have wild nights where she'd pick a theme and serve a dinner centered around a culture she was feeling at the time. Whenever "Russian Night" rolled through she'd make Borscht Oxtail with Sausage or a Yam Stroganoff. I loved the stroganoff when she made it with short ribs. I've updated this yam recipe by adding lamb, but the true essence and original flavors are rep'd, so kick back and enjoy it with a glass of vodka, just like they do in Russia.

SERVES **6 to 8**   PREP AND COOKING TIME **1 hour, 10 minutes**

YAMS
3 tbsps. unsalted butter
3 tbsps. dark brown sugar
½ tsp. pure vanilla extract
1 tbsp. pure maple syrup
¼ cup water
  A pinch of sea salt
2 large yams, peeled and
  sliced into 1-in. cubes
  (wedges are OK too)

LAMB
2 tbsps. black peppercorns,
  crushed
1 to 2 tbsps. granulated garlic
1 tbsp. dried chives,
  crushed by hand

2 tbsps. all-purpose flour
1 tsp. sea salt
3 lbs. boneless lamb stew meat,
  cut into 1-in. cubes
2 tbsps. olive oil
2 tbsps. canola oil

SAUCE
1 tbsp. unsalted butter
1 tbsp. olive oil
3 shallots, finely chopped
1 green bell pepper, ribs and
  seeds removed, minced
  Celery leaves from 1 bunch,
  minced (optional)
½ lb. mushrooms of your choosing,
  wiped clean and sliced

¼ cup vodka
⅛ tsp. freshly ground nutmeg
  A few pinches chopped
  fresh tarragon
½ cup sour cream,
  at room temperature
2 cups heavy whipping cream
  Sea salt and freshly ground
  black pepper

NOODLES
1 lb. egg noodles
2 tbsps. olive oil
  Shaved Parmesan

MAKE THE YAMS
1. Preheat oven to 375°F.
2. In a small baking dish or pie plate, add the butter, brown sugar, vanilla, and maple syrup. Add water and salt, stir, and then add the yams. Bake the yams until caramelized, basting them occasionally, about 35 minutes. Set aside.

MAKE THE LAMB

1. In a small bowl, combine the peppercorns, granulated garlic, chives, flour, and salt.
2. Rub the lamb with the olive oil, and dredge in the spice flour mixture.
3. In 12-inch sauté pan set on medium-high, heat the canola oil until shimmering. Sear the lamb until brown on all sides, about 3 minutes per side. Transfer the seared lamb to a bowl and set aside.

MAKE THE SAUCE

1. In same pan on medium, heat butter and olive oil. Add the shallots, bell peppers, and celery leaves, if using. Cook for 3 minutes. Add the mushrooms and cook, stirring occasionally, for 4 minutes more.
2. Remove pan from heat and carefully deglaze it with the vodka. Add the nutmeg and tarragon, stirring to combine.
3. Reduce the heat to low and add the sour cream and heavy cream. Add a tablespoon or two of water if sauce is too thick. Stir in the candied yams and a tablespoon of the butter-syrup from the baking dish. Add more to taste. Add the lamb and simmer on low until the sauce has thickened, about 10 to 15 minutes. Season with salt and pepper to taste.

MAKE THE NOODLES

Cook the egg noodles al dente according to the directions on the package. Drain, return noodles to pot, and toss with the olive oil. Keep warm until ready to serve.

SERVE

In individual dishes, serve meat-and-potato sauce on top of the noodles. Garnish with ground nutmeg, pepper, shaved Parmesan, and minced tarragon. Accompany with some mixed greens dressed with your favorite vinaigrette.

CAJUN SMOKED TEA DUCK

I used to go fishing with my uncle, and I remember thinking it was dope getting up at three in the morning and wearing a fresh fishing vest with all my favorite band buttons and punk chains attached—I felt like a superhero. When it came to hunting (i.e., shooting animals), though, it wasn't for me. My uncle would bring back deer, possum, and snakes from his hunting trips for adult-only dishes. The closest we kids ever got to game was duck at the Chinese restaurant! It was PG-13 compared to my uncle's R-rated haul, but we loved it. We'd order smoked duck with all those awesome condiments. I remember being perplexed by the crazy spice of it. Years later, I realized that what I had tasted was flavors created by the Chinese tea-smoking technique. You can rep those flavors here either with a smoker or by using a grill.

SERVES **4**   PREP AND COOKING TIME **6 to 7 hours, plus overnight marinating**

1 5-1b. duck

RUB

4 tsps. salt
2 tsps. Chinese Five Spice powder
1 tsp. ground ginger
1 tsp. white sugar
1 tsp. ground coriander
1½ tbsps. paprika
1 tsp. cornstarch
1 tsp. garlic powder
1 tsp. onion powder
   A pinch of dried thyme
1 tsp. freshly ground black pepper
1 tsp. cayenne pepper
   A pinch of dried basil
1 tsp. sesame oil
   A pinch of dried oregano

CAVITY MIX

   A few slivers fresh ginger
1 orange, sliced into 8 wedges
4 garlic cloves, 1 sliced and
   3 smashed with skin on
3 shallots, halved, skin on
1 apple, cored and sliced
   into 8 wedges
1 cinnamon stick

SMOKE POUCH

(Double this to make 2 pouches
for an intense smoked flavor)
2 cups loose tea leaves (Chinese
   black, green, lavender, chamomile,
   or a combo)

¼ cup light brown sugar, packed
¼ cup white rice
   Grated zest of ½ orange
10 whole star anise
2 cinnamon sticks
1 tbsp. cumin seeds
1 tbsp. fennel seeds
1 tbsp. caraway seeds

GLAZE

1 to 2 tbsps. sesame oil
¼ cup honey
   Splash of amino acids, preferably
   Bragg's, or soy sauce

SPECIAL EQUIPMENT

   Heavy-duty aluminum foil
   Smoker
   Kitchen torch

DAY 1: PREP THE DUCK

1. Fill a large teakettle or stock pot with cold water and bring it to a boil.
2. Meanwhile, with the tip of a paring knife, pierce the skin of the duck in 1-inch intervals. Only go as deep as the skin and fat layer, don't poke the meat; when you feel resistance, you've hit the flesh—stop.

DOUBLE UP

I've found that using two smoke pouches really infuses flavor into the meat. I add the second pouch after the duck has been smoking for an hour.

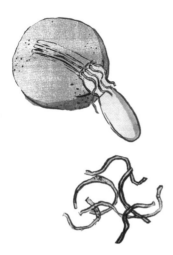

3. Place duck in your very clean sink, and slowly and carefully pour half the boiling water over breast side of the duck. Repeat on back side. Dry duck with paper towels and set aside.

4. In a small bowl, combine all of the rub ingredients except sesame oil. Rub duck with sesame oil, then cover completely with the rub. Season cavity as well.

5. Stuff the duck with the ginger, orange, garlic, shallots, apple wedges, and cinnamon stick.

6. Place duck on a pan or platter, cover with plastic film, and refrigerate at least overnight, or up to 3 days.

DAY 2: SMOKE THE DUCK

1. Take duck out of refrigerator and let it come to room temperature (about 45 minutes).

2. If you have a smoker, set it up according to the manufacturer's instructions and preheat it to 275°F. If you are using a grill, see page 24 for directions.

3. In a small bowl, combine all smoke pouch ingredients. Make a 3 x 4-inch foil pouch with heavy-duty foil or two or three layers of regular foil. Poke holes in the top of the pouch so the smoke can escape. Place smoke mixture in pouch and set aside (see Note).

4. Place duck, breast-side down, on a grate with a drip pan positioned underneath it. Put smoke pouch on or near the hot coals. Smoke duck for 4 to 6 hours at 225°F to 275°F.

5. During the final 30 minutes of smoking, prepare the glaze. In a sauce pan set on medium heat, add the sesame oil, honey, and aminos or soy sauce. Heat until honey is melted, about 3 minutes. Keep warm.

6. Remove duck from the smoker or grill, and place on a heat-safe platter. Brush the glaze over the duck. Break out your kitchen torch and crisp the skin by running a medium flame evenly over the bird, being careful not to stay in one spot too long. Torch until skin reaches desired crispiness.

7. Allow duck to rest for 15 minutes, then carve by first removing the legs and wings. Next, slice the two breasts off whole, then slice breast meat into smaller portions. The smoked duck is awesome served with some lettuce, cucumbers, Blueberry-Guinness BBQ Sauce (page 204), and crêpes, or try it as a taco filling.

SPICY STRAWBERRY ~~BABY BACKS~~

Although I don't eat crazy amounts of pork, I have a straight-up weakness for pork baby back ribs. My condition is so serious that I can't ever be around them—I'll easily devour two slabs by myself—so when I make this dish I make sure to have lots of people around to chow down. Incredulous about combining strawberries and ribs? The inspiration came from the strawberries my grandmother had in her backyard, which would smell like BBQ every weekend because of her smokers. This dish is moderately time consuming to make (the ribs have to be smoked ahead of time) but it has unfussy prep and is super delicious. Depending on the size of your crowd, I recommend doing at least three batches for a main course—they go quickly. You can caramelize them a few different ways—with a gas or charcoal grill, smoker, or even a kitchen torch.

SERVES **4 (½ slab per person)**   PREP AND COOKING TIME **6 hours, plus 1 to 24 hours for marinating**

2 slabs of ribs (see Note)
3 tbsps. canola oil
6 oz. freeze-dried strawberries, ground
8 tbsps. DFC BBQ Meat Rub (page 191)

Blueberry-Guinness BBQ Sauce (page 204) or your favorite BBQ sauce

RIB PREP NOTE

If the butcher hasn't already taken care of this: trim the fat and remove the tough silver skin from the top of the ribs. The silver skin is the membrane that is attached to the back of the rib bones; it will prevent the smoke and any rub flavorings from penetrating the meat. It needs to go! Just peel it off with a knife at the corner, and then use your fingers to rip the whole thing off.

SPICE THE RIBS

1. Rinse the ribs in cool water and pat them dry with paper towels. Place ribs on a platter or in a casserole dish and coat them with the oil.
2. In a small bowl, combine the ground strawberries with the rub.
3. Sprinkle the rub, about 2 tablespoons per side depending on the size of the slabs, to coat the ribs. Rub it in. Cover platter or dish with plastic wrap and refrigerate the ribs for 1 hour, or up to overnight.

BBQ THE RIBS

Set up a smoker (page 24) and preheat to 225°F. Position the ribs above your drip pan, and cook them for 3 to 4 hours, depending on the thickness of the ribs. To check for doneness, use the bend test (aka the bounce test). Using tongs, pick up a slab and bend or bounce it gently. If the surface cracks, the ribs are ready.

 **CARAMELIZING RIBS**

On a charcoal grill,
position the coated slab
directly over the coals.
On a gas grill, remove the
water pan and crank up
all the burners. On a water
smoker, remove the
water pan and move the
meat close to the coals.

GLAZE THE RIBS
Brush both sides of the slabs with Blueberry-Guinness BBQ Sauce, and move slabs directly over the hottest part of the grill to caramelize and crisp the sauce (see Note). Stand by, the sweet sauce goes from caramelized to carbonized in less than a minute! One coat of sauce should be enough, but if you need two, go ahead, but no more! Serve the ribs with the remaining sauce on the side—or skip the sauce if you prefer.

DFC STEAK PIE

DISH IT!

I'm fascinated with the UK—it's the birthparent of America and a second home to me because of my friends there, whom I refer to as my London fam. Naturally, our cultures have a lot in common and it turns out this ultimate pie, which I thought was the epitome of American classics, is actually a UK original. But DFC does it differently: instead of using a Guinness base, I braise the steak in chocolate-laced wine, shoot the crust through with toasted poppy seeds, and top it with cracked black pepper. Cheers.

SERVES **4 to 6**   PREP AND COOKING TIME **2 hours**

FILLING

- 2 lbs. boneless beef chuck, cut into 1-in. pieces
- 2 tbsps. all-purpose flour
- ¼ tsp. baking powder
- 1 tsp. sea salt
- ½ tsp. freshly ground black pepper
- 2 tbsps. canola oil
- 3 tbsps. water
- 1 large yellow onion, coarsely chopped
- 3 garlic cloves, 2 chopped and 1 minced
- 2 carrots, diced
- 2 celery stalks, diced

- 1 red bell pepper, ribs and seeds removed, diced
- 1½ tbsps. tomato paste
- 1 cup Chicken or Veggie Stock (pages 194–195)
- 1 cup chocolate wine or 1 square baking chocolate
- 1 tbsp. amino acids, preferably Bragg's
- 2 tsps. ground black peppercorns
- 2 sprigs fresh rosemary
- 2 bay leaves
- 1 15.5-oz. can white or lima beans, drained
- 3 large sweet potatoes, peeled and diced

- ½ cup frozen peas, thawed
- 1 cup grated extra-sharp aged Cheddar cheese

CRUST

- 1 Orange Coconilla pie crust recipe (page 153), omit the orange zest and orange juice
- 1 tbsp. toasted poppy seeds
- 1 tsp. turmeric
- ½ tsp. curry powder
- 1 large egg, lightly beaten
- 1 tbsp. water

MAKE THE FILLING

1. Place oven rack in the middle position and preheat oven to 350°F.
2. Rinse beef and pat dry.
3. In a shallow dish, combine the flour, baking powder, salt, and pepper. Add the beef, turning to coat, then shake off the excess and transfer to a plate.
4. In a 6-quart ovenproof pot or Dutch oven set on medium-high, heat the canola oil until shimmering. Sear the beef in 3 batches, browning on all sides, about 5 minutes per batch. Transfer seared beef to a bowl.
5. Deglaze pot with the water, scraping up brown bits. Add the onion, garlic, carrots, celery, and bell pepper, stirring frequently, until onion is softened, about 5 minutes. Add the tomato paste and cook, stirring constantly, 1 minute.

6. Add beef with any juices accumulated in bowl, broth, chocolate wine (or chocolate), amino acids, peppercorns, rosemary, bay leaves, and bring to a simmer. Cover and transfer to oven.

7. Braise until beef is very tender and sauce is thickened, about 1 to 1½ hours. Add the beans in the last 30 minutes of braising.

8. Discard rosemary and bay leaves, and cool stew, uncovered, for 30 minutes.

9. Meanwhile, cook the sweet potatoes in a large stock pot until tender, about 20 to 25 minutes. Drain and mash them with a little butter or olive oil. Fold in the peas and Cheddar. Set aside.

MAKE THE CRUST

1. Make the crust (page 153), including the additional ingredients listed (except the egg and water), through step 4. Separate the dough into two balls, wrap each in plastic film, and refrigerate for 30 minutes. Preheat the oven to 375°F.

2. On a lightly floured surface, roll out one dough ball into a circle about 11 inches in diameter and ⅛ inch thick. To transfer to the pie dish, carefully wrap dough around rolling pin and center it above an ungreased, 9-inch pie dish. Carefully unroll dough onto the pie dish, and gently press the dough into the dish. Trim the excess dough. Freeze the crust for 10 minutes.

3. Line the crust with foil or parchment, leaving a 1-inch overhang. Fill with pie weights or dried beans, and bake until the edges of the crust start to brown, about 20 minutes. Remove the weights and foil, and return the crust to the oven to bake for 10 more minutes. Set the crust on a wire rack to cool completely. Lower the oven temperature to 350°F.

4. When pie shell is cool, use a slotted spoon to fill the pie shell with stew. Add more gravy as desired. Top the stew with the mashed sweet potatoes.

5. Roll out the second dough ball in a 9 x 11-inch rectangle. Cut strips for a lattice top for the pie. It doesn't have to look perfect; in fact, it should look kinda bootleg rustic.

6. Combine the egg and water, and with pastry brush paint the lattice and crust edges with egg wash. Top it with a little cracked black pepper if you like.

BAKE UP

Bake the pie until the crust is golden brown, about 20 to 30 minutes. Serve with winter greens tossed with a simple vinaigrette.

PUMPKIN PATCH* FISH-N-CHIPS

London is the king of fish and chips, and I always dip into this national dish when I'm there. The traditional UK recipe is a very bare-bones process. What's incredible, though, is how many different fish shops exist and how passionate people are about their local variety. I developed this recipe after I learned the British way of F-n-C; then I flipped it by creating a super-light, pumpkin-spiced beer batter. Add a side of yucca chips drowned in CocoNana Curry Ketchup and Boujee Ranch Sauce and you've got awesomeness on a plate.

SERVES **6 as an entrée or 9 tapas style**   PREP AND COOKING TIME **1 hour**

4 large yucca or cassava roots, peeled, cored, and cut into large pieces
3 lbs. white flaky fish (tilapia, pollock, or cod), cut into 1-in. pieces

BATTER
4 cups all-purpose flour
1 ½ tbsps. baking powder
2 tsps. kosher salt

A pinch of cayenne pepper
A pinch of celery seed
A pinch of cinnamon
A pinch of ground ginger
A pinch of garlic powder
A pinch of onion powder
A pinch of ground cumin
1 tbsp. minced fresh sage leaves
1 to 2 12-oz. bottles dark beer
1 tbsp. unsalted butter, melted
1 cup cornstarch

4 tbsps. canned or frozen pumpkin or squash purée
1 gallon safflower oil

SPECIAL EQUIPMENT
Candy thermometer

COOK THE YUCCA
1. Preheat oven to 200°F.
2. Bring a large stock pot of salted water to a boil and cook the yucca until it starts to turn translucent and can be pierced easily with a fork, about 20 to 30 minutes. Drain thoroughly.
3. Check yucca for any remaining fibrous pieces and remove them. Cut into 1-inch-thick wedges. Set aside.

MAKE THE BATTER
1. In a large bowl, combine the flour, baking powder, salt, cayenne, celery seed, cinnamon, ground ginger, garlic powder, onion powder, and cumin.
2. In a blender, purée 12 ounces of the beer, butter, and pumpkin or squash until smooth. The consistency should be loose. Add more beer if mixture is too thick.

3. Add the pumpkin purée to the spiced flour, mixing until batter is completely smooth and free of lumps. Add more beer (1 tablespoon at a time) if batter is too thick. Cover and refrigerate 15 minutes to 1 hour.

COAT AND FRY THE FISH

1. Before you start coating and frying, set up your work area. See Get Set Up (page 33) for instructions.

2. Prepare a deep fryer according to the instructions or fill a high-sided, heavy-bottomed 12-inch skillet (preferably cast-iron) halfway with oil (about 3 inches) set on high and heat the oil to 350°F. Check the oil temperature with a candy thermometer.

3. While oil heats, put the cornstarch in a dish. Lightly dredge each fish piece and set the coated fish on a wire rack.

4. Working in small batches, dip fish pieces into the batter, and then gently slip them in the hot oil. Fry 4 to 6 minutes, turning halfway through. The fish should be golden brown, and internal temperature should be 140°F.

5. Drain fish on a wire rack set inside a baking sheet. Keep warm in preheated oven while you fry the yucca.

FRY THE YUCCA

Check oil temperature and raise the heat if it is not 350°F. Working in batches, fry yucca wedges, turning occasionally, until golden brown, about 5 minutes. Carefully remove the yucca from the oil with a slotted spoon and drain on a wire rack or on a plate lined with newspapers or paper towels.

SERVE

Sprinkle fried yucca with sea salt and serve with the fried fish, CocoNana Curry Ketchup (page 201), and Boujee Ranch Sauce (page 200).

DRUNK-N-FRUITY PULLED PORK
WITH CHERRY PECAN SAUCE

I first made this dish in London, where I had to smoke hundreds of pounds of pork shoulder at the Notting Hill Carnival, the most epic party I've ever done. London's Caribbean community freaked out over this dish, as they should have—its base spices are totally island inspired. It was a massive hit! There are similarities here to jerk pork—the Jamaican spice rub and grilling technique—but it's got its own distinct flavor (no disrespect).

SERVES **12 to 14**   PREP AND COOKING TIME **10 minutes, plus 10 hours for smoking**

- 1 5-lb. boneless pork butt, fat cap trimmed, tied with butcher's twine
- 3 tbsps. vegetable oil
- ⅓ cup DFC BBQ Meat Rub (page 191)
- 2 cups wood chips, such as cherry maple or apple

CHERRY PECAN SAUCE

- 1 cup dried sour cherries
- 1 cup whiskey, preferably Jameson

- ½ cup crushed toasted pecans
- 1 8-oz. can of pineapple chunks, drained
- 2 cups yellow mustard
- ⅔ cup apple cider vinegar, preferably Bragg's
- 3 tbsps. tomato paste
- ½ tsp. Sriracha or your favorite hot sauce
- 2 tsps. miso paste
- ¾ cup light brown sugar, packed

- 2 tsps. dried rosemary leaves
- 1 tsp. celery seed
- 3 tsps. ground mustard
- 2 tsps. onion powder
- 2 tsps. garlic powder
- 1 tsp. sea salt
- 1 tsp. freshly ground black pepper

SPECIAL EQUIPMENT
- Smoker
- Meat claws

HOW TO SOFTEN TOUGH PORK

Sometimes you will get a butt that, even after 6 hours of smoking, is still tough. Transfer it to a roasting pan, pour 12 ounces of beer over it, cover with aluminum foil, and bake at 300°F for 1 to 2 hours until the meat is falling apart.

DAY 1: COAT THE PORK

In a large bowl or shallow dish, coat the pork with the oil. Rub in the spice mix, cover the bowl or dish with plastic wrap, and refrigerate overnight.

DAY 2: SMOKE THE PORK

1. The next day, set up a smoker and preheat it to 225°F (see page 24). Smoke the pork for 6 to 10 hours. The pork is done when the exterior is dark and the internal temperature reaches 190°F. Insert a fork into the pork and twist it 90 degrees. If the meat gives and pulls away easy, it's done (see Note).

2. When pork is done and cooled down, it's time to pull the pork. You can take two large forks and get to shredding, but the BBQ tool called *meat claws* helps shred meat more quickly and efficiently.

COOK UP
WITH FRUIT

Because of my grandmother's ways when I was growing up, I never thought it was unusual to pair fruit with savory dishes. It wasn't until I ate at friends' houses and wondered aloud, "Why aren't there any cranberries in the coleslaw?" and they'd be all, "WTF?!" that I realized my family's cooking was different from the mainstream. The savory-fruit combination—outside of the classics like pork and apple or duck and orange—just doesn't appear in Southern cooking. In Mediterranean and African cuisine, however, dried fruits are a staple—the practice started when they'd dry and store berries and then rehydrate them for eating in winter, usually as a natural sweetener in stews.

MAKE THE SAUCE

1. While the pork is in the smoker, in a medium bowl, mix together the cherries, whiskey, pecans, pineapple, mustard, tomato paste, Sriracha, miso paste, and brown sugar.

2. Crush the rosemary leaves and celery seed in a mortar and pestle or in a spice grinder. Add it to the whiskey mixture. Stir in the ground mustard, onion powder, garlic powder, salt, and pepper, and mix thoroughly. Refrigerate the mixture for 1 hour.

3. Transfer the chilled mixture to a medium sauce pan set on low, and simmer the sauce for 20 minutes. Serve alongside the pulled pork. Leftover sauce will keep in the fridge, in an airtight container, for up to 1 month.

SERVE

Toss pulled pork with Cherry Pecan Sauce and serve on buns, with rice or bread, or just straight up.

MANGO-COCONUT SHRIMP

I've been making this recipe for years—it's one of the first seafood dishes I introduced to the public at my DFC parties, where it became a major hit. It was inspired by Mexican street vendors and their bags of sliced mango seasoned with salt, lime, and chili—I love that stuff, and I knew it would work well with seafood. Take succulent shrimp, deep fry it, add the mango chili sauce, and then top it with lime, toasted coconut, chili flakes, and shredded, unripe (green) mango. Serve it up, and the insane combination of freshness and spice will have 'em clamoring for more.

SERVES **6 as an entrée or 12 tapas style**   PREP AND COOKING TIME **1 ½ hours**

3 lbs. jumbo or large shrimp, peeled and deveined, tails on

MANGO SAUCE
2 dried ancho chilies (see Note)
2 to 3 cups water
2 garlic cloves, smashed
2 serrano chilies, ribs and seeds removed, diced
½ tsp. sea salt, plus more to taste
½ tsp. ground cloves

ANCHO NOTE

Ancho chilies are sometimes called *pasilla* in the United States.

TAKE CARE

When working with chilies, wear protective gloves or wash your hands very thoroughly with soap and warm water after handling them. Do not touch or rub your eyes while you are handling chili peppers.

1 tbsp. unsalted butter
¼ cup mango preserves
1 tbsp. honey
1 squirt Sriracha (optional)

TOPPING
1 cup coconut flakes
2 green (unripe) mangoes
  Red pepper flakes
  Lime wedges

WET BATTER
½ cup coconut milk
1 large egg, well beaten

COATING
1 cup rolled oats
½ cup all-purpose flour
½ tsp. baking powder
½ cup yellow cornmeal
⅓ tsp. sea salt
½ tsp. white pepper
1 tbsp. Old Bay or DFC Fish Fry Spice Mix (page 189)
½ cup unsweetened large-flake coconut
4 cups peanut or canola oil

SPECIAL EQUIPMENT
Candy thermometer

MAKE THE SAUCE

1. Using a paring knife, cut a slit down the center of each ancho chili. Remove the stems, ribs, and seeds. Reserve a few seeds and ribs if you want to add heat to the sauce (see Note).

2. In a 10-inch skillet set on medium-high, press the chilies into the skillet, insides down, and warm them for a few seconds. Turn chilies over and warm a few seconds more, being careful not to toast or burn them.

3. Add enough water to the skillet to just cover the chilies. Bring to a boil, then remove from heat and let sit, uncovered, until chilies are soft and plump, about 10 minutes.

4. Remove the chilies from the pan, reserving the water. Place chilies in a blender, along with the garlic, serrano, salt, ground cloves, and 1½ cups of water from the skillet. Purée until smooth, about 1 minute. Taste the sauce and adjust the seasoning with salt. If you want more heat, add a few of the reserved pepper seeds or ribs, and purée again. Discard any unused water.

5. Transfer the sauce to the skillet. Add the butter, preserves, honey, and Sriracha, if using. Bring to a simmer on medium, then reduce heat to maintain a low simmer for 10 minutes. Skim off any foam that rises to the top. Remove the skillet from the heat. Reheat the sauce while you're frying the shrimp.

MAKE THE TOPPING

1. Preheat oven to 350°F. Spread the coconut flakes in a single layer on a baking sheet and toast until golden brown, 5 to 8 minutes. Remove from oven and set aside in a small bowl.

2. Using a sharp paring knife, peel the mangoes.

3. Using a medium-size to large box grater, grate the mangoes into a medium bowl, mind the pit. Set the grated mango aside with the toasted coconut until you're ready to serve the shrimp.

COAT THE SHRIMP

1. Before you start coating and frying, set up your work area. See Get Set Up (page 33) for instructions.

2. Season the shrimp with a pinch each of salt and pepper, and let them stand at room temperature for 10 to 15 minutes.

3. In a medium bowl, combine the half and half or coconut milk and the beaten egg.

4. In another medium bowl, combine the coating ingredients.

5. With one hand, dip each shrimp in the egg mixture, letting the excess drip off. With the other, "dry," hand, dig a well in the flour mixture and gently bury the shrimp. Lift it out by the tail and place it on a wire rack set over newspaper or paper towels. Repeat until all the shrimp are coated.

FRY THE SHRIMP

1. Prepare a deep fryer according to the instructions or fill a high-sided, heavy-bottomed 10-inch skillet (preferably cast-iron) halfway with oil (about 2 inches) set on high and heat the oil to 350°F. Check the oil temperature with a candy thermometer.

2. Working in batches, fry the shrimp until light golden brown, about 2 minutes per side. As they come out of the oil, place them on the rack to drain.

3. Using tongs, dip each fried shrimp into the simmering sauce and top them with a mound of shredded mango, some toasted coconut, and a sprinkle of red pepper flakes. Serve the shrimp with lime wedges and Boujee Ranch Sauce (page 200).

▼SMOTHERED▲
SARDINES -N- TOAST

The first time I had chanterelle mushrooms on toast, I freaked out it was so good. Same with the UK's sardines and toast—I'm talking, YUM! So one day it hit me: what if these dishes got down with each other? Somebody 'bout to get pregnant! This is their ultimate offspring: a combination of homemade yeast toast with cornmeal-coated fried sardines smothered in chanterelle gravy topped with roasted okra, a fried egg, and shaved Cheddar. Try it after a night out—it's the most decadent hangover remedy ever.

SERVES **4 as an entrée or 8 tapas-style**   PREP AND COOKING TIME **2 hours**

TOAST
- 2 tbsps. black sesame seeds
- 1 tbsp. white sugar
- 1 package dry yeast (about 2 ¼ tsps.)
- 1 cup whole milk, warmed to 100°F to 110°F
- 3 tbsps. unsalted butter, melted and cooled

BREAD NOTE

When making bread, it should be a warm day or in a hot kitchen so the yeast activates—yeast loves warm, moist environments. When baking bread in the winter or on cool days, turn your oven to the lowest setting for 20 minutes and place a large pot of water inside the oven. Once you've mixed your bread dough, turn off the oven, remove the pot of water, and set dough bowl in the center of the stove to rise, about 1 to 2 hours. You can make this bread 2 to 3 days in advance of use, just keep it in an airtight container.

- 3 ¼ cups all-purpose flour
- 1 tsp. sea salt
  Cooking spray or olive oil

OKRA AND SARDINES
- 16 okra
- 2 tbsps. canola oil
  Sea salt
- 1 cup all-purpose flour
  A pinch of baking powder
- ½ cup white cornmeal

- 1 tsp. Old Bay or DFC Fish Fry Spice Mix (page 189)
- 8 fresh sardine fillets
- 2 cups peanut or canola oil
  Do or Die Bed-Stuy Shepherd's Pie gravy, hot (page 64)

SPECIAL EQUIPMENT
  5 x 9-inch loaf pan
  Candy thermometer

MAKE THE BREAD (see Note)
1. Preheat oven to 375°F.
2. Arrange the sesame seeds on a baking sheet and toast until fragrant, about 6 minutes. Put toasted seeds on a cutting board and crush them with the underside of a frying pan or a rolling pin. Scoop crushed seeds into a small bowl, and set aside.
3. In a large bowl, dissolve the sugar and yeast in the warm milk; let mixture stand for 5 minutes.
4. Stir in 2 tablespoons of the butter and all of the sesame seeds.
5. Add 3 cups of the flour and the salt to yeast mixture, stirring with a spoon until a soft dough forms.
6. Turn dough onto a floured surface and knead it until smooth and elastic, about 8 minutes. Add remaining ¼ cup flour, 1 tablespoon at a time, to prevent dough from sticking to your hands.
7. Place dough in a large bowl coated with cooking spray or olive oil, turning to coat. Cover with plastic wrap or a dish towel and let rise in a warm, draft-free place (about 85°F) for 1 hour, or until

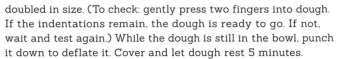

doubled in size. (To check: gently press two fingers into dough. If the indentations remain, the dough is ready to go. If not, wait and test again.) While the dough is still in the bowl, punch it down to deflate it. Cover and let dough rest 5 minutes.

8. On a lightly floured surface, roll dough into a 14 x 7-inch rectangle. Tightly roll up the rectangle, starting with a short edge. Press firmly to eliminate air pockets, pinching seam and ends to seal.

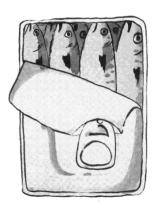

9. Place dough roll, seam side down, in a loaf pan coated with cooking spray. Lightly coat top of dough with cooking spray, and cover with a clean kitchen towel or plastic wrap. Let rise in a warm, draft-free place (85°F) 30 minutes, or until doubled in size.

10. Preheat oven to 400°F.

11. Uncover dough and drizzle surface with remaining 1 table-spoon butter, gently spreading with a pastry brush. Using a sharp knife, cut a 1/4-inch-deep slit lengthwise down center of the dough loaf. Bake 30 minutes, or until bread is browned on top and sounds hollow when tapped. Turn the bread out of the loaf pan (use a knife to loosen it if the sides are stuck, and set the bread on a wire rack to cool.

ROAST THE OKRA

1. Preheat oven to 350°F.

2. Meanwhile, toss the okra with the oil and salt to taste. Arrange in a single layer on a rimmed baking sheet and roast until browned, about 20 minutes. Keep warm while you fry the sardines.

COAT AND FRY THE SARDINES

1. Before coating and frying the sardines, prepare your work area. See Get Set Up (page 33) for instructions.

2. In a shallow plate, combine the flour, baking powder, cornmeal, and Old Bay or DFC Fish Fry Spice Mix.

3. Dredge sardines in the flour mixture, and place them on a wire rack to let the coating set.

4. Meanwhile, prepare your deep fryer according to the instructions or fill a high-sided, heavy bottomed 10-inch frying pan (preferably cast-iron) halfway with the oil and heat on medium to 350°F. Check the oil temperature with a candy thermometer.

5. Gently place coated sardines in the hot oil and fry 8 to 10 minutes, turning halfway through. Internal temperature of the sardines should be 140°F.

6. Carefully remove sardines from oil and drain on a wire rack or on newspaper or paper towels.

SERVE

1. Slice bread into 8 1-inch-thick slices, then toast.

2. Place 2 pieces of toast in each of 4 plates. Ladle some Do or Die gravy onto the toast, then top each with a sardine. Add a little more gravy and place 4 pieces of okra next to each sardine.

SOCK-IT-TO-ME STIR~FRY

I've never had a stir-fry as good as my grandmother's Sock-It-to-Me version. She not only put her heart and soul into this dish, she put her whole body into it. I've included a choice of proteins here so you can do it up any way you like. Or, you can skip the meat step altogether—if you go veggie, just follow the rest of the recipe and add a teaspoon of sesame oil. I'm not going to waste any more words on this recipe since I don't want to hold you up: it's so incredible, you should be making it right now!

SERVES **4 to 6**   PREP AND COOKING TIME **45 minutes, plus 30 minutes to overnight marinating**

CHOOSE YOUR PROTEIN (1 OR MORE!):
1 lb. boneless, skinless chicken breast, thinly sliced into bite-size pieces **or**
1 ½ lbs. top sirloin steak, thinly sliced (freeze the steak for 30 minutes for easier cutting) **or**
1 lb. veggie protein or seitan **or**
3 pieces twice-fried tofu or bean curd, smoked tofu, braised tofu, or firm tofu, cubed or sliced **or**
1 ½ lbs. pork belly, braised and chopped **or**
1 lb. shrimp, shelled and deveined

MARINADE FOR PROTEIN
2 tbsps. amino acids, preferably Bragg's
1 tbsp. Chinese rice wine or dry sherry
¼ tsp. sesame oil
4 tbsps. peanut or canola oil

VEGGIES
1 tbsp. cornstarch
¼ cup water
1 garlic clove, crushed and chopped
1 fennel bulb, cored and sliced
1 thumb-size piece of fresh ginger, peeled and thinly sliced
½ lb. snap peas, fibrous stems removed
½ cup almonds, toasted
¼ lb. oyster mushrooms, wiped clean and sliced
2 carrots, julienned
1 red bell pepper, ribs and seeds removed, julienned
1 celery stalk, thinly sliced
1 leek, white parts only, thinly sliced and washed
1 to 3 dried Thai chilies (or your favorite chili)
2 green onions, white and green parts sliced diagonally (optional)
1 cup (about half of a 15-oz. can) baby corn, drained
3 collard green leaves, de-stemmed and finely chopped
1 lb. broccoli, stems removed, quartered
1 8-oz. can of water chestnuts or bamboo shoots

1 15.5-oz. can black-eyed peas, drained
1 sweet potato, peeled, cubed, and steamed
½ cup chopped fresh pineapple
8 cherry tomatoes, halved
5 black peppercorns, whole
8 okra, roasted and halved (optional; see Note)
Cilantro to taste (optional)

SAUCE
2 to 3 tbsps. amino acids, preferably Bragg's
1 tbsp. cooking wine or beer Juices from the stir-fried protein
1 tbsp. plum jelly
A pinch of Chinese Five Spice powder
½ tsp. vegetable bouillon
2 tbsps. vegetarian oyster sauce

SPECIAL EQUIPMENT
Wok

~~~~~

MARINATE YOUR PROTEIN

Add protein and marinade ingredients to 1-gallon Ziploc bag, shake it up, seal, and refrigerate for 30 minutes or up to overnight. If using braised pork belly, marinate for just 30 minutes.

START STIR-FRYING

1. In a large cast-iron skillet or wok, heat 2 tablespoons of the oil. As oil heats, separate your protein into small batches no larger than what can fit into the palm of your hand. Stir-fry chicken until no longer pink, about 3 to 5 minutes; beef will take 2 minutes for rare; cook veggie proteins for 2 to 3 minutes; the pork belly and shrimp, 3 minutes. Transfer cooked protein and juices to a bowl, and set aside.

2. Add remaining oil to skillet or wok and heat until it starts to smoke slightly.

3. While the oil is heating, quickly mix the cornstarch and water until completely combined, and set aside.

4. When oil is ready, start stir-frying a few veggies at a time, beginning with those that take longer to cook: broccoli, celery, garlic, ginger, fennel, pineapple, tomatoes, green onions, carrots, bell peppers, and leeks. Stir-fry veggie batches 4 to 5 minutes each, or until crisp tender.

5. Next add the baby corn, water chestnuts, yams, and okra (if using). Give it a good toss and add cornstarch mixture.

6. Pour in all the remaining sauce ingredients, and return your protein to skillet or wok. Continue to cook, stirring frequently until the sauce thickens, about 5 minutes.

SERVE

Serve the stir-fry over rice, egg noodles, chow mein, crispy noodles, or any grain you like. Or forget the grains—it stands up on its own. Garnish with cilantro, if desired.

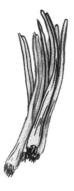

HOW TO ROAST OKRA

To roast okra, preheat oven to 350°F. In a medium bowl, toss the okra with 1 tablespoon olive oil and season to taste with salt and pepper. Roast for 15 minutes, or until slightly crispy. Let cool, then chop the okra into 1-inch pieces.

GUINNESS BBQ BRISKET

Recipes for barbecue sauce and marinades are closely guarded personal secrets in my family. Luckily for you, lil' Dante always stayed up to snoop on everyone's secret ingredients so that I could grow up to be the reigning brisket champ! I would hide behind a chair for hours to watch my uncle put in his secret ingredients: beer and apple sauce. All that detective work resulted in a dish people have loved all around the world. The rich, chocolate-infused, spicy, velvety fruitiness made one Swedish party-goer scream: "This brisket's having sex with me!" I don't know about all that, but this is definitely one of my favorite dishes to make. Like much of my food, this one integrates elements of Korean and Chinese cooking to give it extra flair. My Asian fans have told me the brisket reminds them of the family-style barbecue dishes they grew up with. It's great in a taco, biscuit, dinner roll, bread, over rice, or even eaten by itself.

SERVES **8 to 10**   PREP AND COOKING TIME **10 hours, plus 24 to 48 hours for marinating**

1 beef brisket, grass-fed,
   choice grade
2 tbsps. canola oil
¼ to ½ cup DFC Meat Rub (page 191)
1½ cups wood chips hickory or
   mesquite

WET RUB

1½ cups yellow mustard
4 tbsps. toasted sesame seeds
1 tsp. amino acids,
   preferably Bragg's
1 12-oz. bottle Guinness stout
1 scallion, chopped
1 cup light brown sugar, packed
2 cups Blueberry-Guinness BBQ
   Sauce (page 204), warm

SPECIAL EQUIPMENT

   Grill or smoker with lots of
   charcoal (the large economy bag
   or two medium bags)
6 feet of heavy-duty aluminum foil
   Pastry brush, preferably silicone
   Meat thermometer
   Alarm clock

PREP THE BRISKET

1. Rinse the meat and dry it with paper towels. If the butcher hasn't already done so, trim off most of the fat cap, leaving at least ¼ inch of fat.

2. Place the meat on a large sheet of aluminum foil, coat the meat lightly with oil, and sprinkle it all over with the dry rub. Massage it in. Let the meat sit for at least 1 to 2 hours to allow the rub to penetrate the meat. A moist paste will form that will become a crust as the meat smokes.

MAKE THE WET RUB

In a medium bowl, combine all of the wet rub ingredients. Once the dry-rubbed meat has set, mop it with the wet rub, using a silicone pastry brush. Wrap the foil around the meat and let it marinate for 24 to 48 hours in the refrigerator.

GRILL THE BRISKET

1. When you're ready to grill, preheat your gas or charcoal grill or smoker. Set it up for indirect cooking and preheat to 225°F. Keep the temperature low, because heating the meat too fast will extract the juices. See page 24 for instructions on how to set up the grill for indirect heat.
2. Put the meat on the grill, fat side up. Add wood as soon as the meat is on the grill. Continue adding wood ⅓ cup at a time every 30 minutes during the first 2 hours, whenever the smoke stops. Smoke the meat for 4 to 6 hours, then transfer the meat to a large roasting pan.
3. Preheat the oven to 250°F.
4. Pour one bottle of beer over the meat, and then add one cup of water to the pan. Cover the pan with foil, and bake the meat for 2 to 4 hours, until the internal temperature is 190°F.

REST, SAUCE, SERVE

1. Remove the meat from the oven and let it rest, covered, for 30 minutes to 1 hour. Reserve ½ cup of the drippings.
2. In a medium sauce pan set on medium, heat the Blueberry-Guinness BBQ Sauce. Stir in the pan drippings and bring to a simmer.
3. When ready to serve, slice the brisket lengthwise. Fold the slices into the BBQ sauce if you like, or serve the sauce on the side.

D'Z ♥ VEGGIE GUMBO

Sabor!

This is a tribute to a classic family dish, and it's also one of the first recipes I mastered in its vegan form during my seven-year stint as a vegan. You may be thinking, *A veggie gumbo? So what, I had that before.* But wait a minute—hold up, fall back, and stay with me. The two problems I have with veggie gumbos are usually as follows: they're made by people who've never had a real gumbo, and they taste like soup. We don't do that here. As with all of my food, we take it mad seriously. Trust me, you've never tasted a veggie gumbo like this before.

SERVES **8 to 10**   PREP AND COOKING TIME **2 hours**

2 tbsps. canola oil
3 spicy tofu sausages, preferably May Wah, sliced into 1-in. pieces
1 lb. tofu nuggets or seitan (page 199), julienned
½ lb. smoked tofu, crumbled
½ cup peanut or canola oil or vegetable shortening
4 to 6 tbsps. flour
1 onion, diced
1 red bell pepper, ribs and seeds removed, diced

½ lb. cherry tomatoes, whole
4 carrots, chopped
2 celery stalks, sliced
3 garlic cloves, minced
½ cup crumbled homemade (page 198) or store-bought tempeh
6 cups Veggie Stock (page 194)
1½ tsp. peanut or almond butter
2 dried bay leaves
1 Old Bay or DFC Fish Fry Spice Mix (page 189)

1½ cups okra, roasted whole, then sliced (see Note)
A dash of amino acids, preferably Bragg's
½ tsp. filé powder (powdered sassafras leaves)
Freshly ground black pepper
Sriracha

HOW TO ROAST OKRA

To roast okra, preheat oven to 350°F. In a medium bowl, toss the okra with 1 tablespoon olive oil and season to taste with salt and pepper. Roast for 15 minutes, or until slightly crispy. Let cool, then chop the okra into 1-inch pieces.

ALL-NATURAL LIQUID AMINOS

Amino acids are the building blocks of life! In liquid form, they are often sold as raw soy sauce (all other soy sauces are fermented), and they are one of my favorite ways to season veggies in place of salt. Aminos are very low in sodium and have tons of Vitamin K and other good-for-ya minerals. They also have a distinct, delicious taste that's tangier, lighter, and fresher than "regular" soy sauce. The brand I prefer is Bragg's, a company founded by health food pioneers in 1912. They make awesome organic apple cider vinegar, too.

For the most part I prefer the straight liquid aminos from Bragg's, but I do use regular soy sauce when I'm making a dope dirty gravy. Now a Southern staple, soy sauce started to become a popular ingredient for gravies in the 1970s as a hassle-free, meat-free alternative to the traditional animal innards that were used to make a proper dirty gravy. The deep, robust flavor that comes from cooking up gizzards, livers, and hearts can now be replaced by a few squirts of soy sauce. No more nasty bits.

GET THE ROUX RIGHT

Your gumbo will taste awful if you don't make the roux properly. The finished roux should be the color of milk chocolate and have a nice toasty smell. If you stop stirring for even one second, the roux will burn.

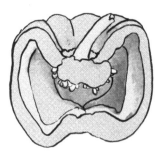

1. In a 6-quart Dutch oven set on medium-high, heat canola oil until shimmering. Add the tofu sausage, tofu nuggets, and smoked tofu, sautéing until brown, about 5 minutes. Transfer to a bowl.

2. In the same pot, add the oil or shortening and heat until hot. Sprinkle the flour into pan and stir constantly for 20 minutes to make a roux. The consistency should be very creamy, like a thinned peanut butter (see Note).

3. Add the onion, bell pepper, tomatoes, carrots, celery, garlic, crumbled tempeh, and smoked tofu to the roux and sauté for about 5 minutes, then crush the tomatoes with back of a wooden spoon.

4. Add the stock, browned tofu, nut butter, bay leaves, and spice mix to the vegetables and bring to a boil, then reduce the heat to low. Cover and simmer for 30 minutes.

5. Remove lid and cook 15 minutes more, stirring occasionally. Add the roasted okra, aminos, and filé powder and let simmer another 15 minutes. Season with black pepper and Sriracha to taste. Serve the gumbo over rice.

VEGAN BLACK SESAME TACOS

This is an insane adaptation of one of our most popular dishes served out of the Ride or Fry truck. I created this dish to come correct for my Veg Heads—they wanted a serious taco too—and I figured out that by grilling the tofu I could get the same growling flavor I get with brisket. Drizzle Blueberry-Guinness BBQ Sauce—or another sauce of your choice—over the tofu to blacken it before serving. These tacos can enliven the scene for any vegetarian at a barbecue.

SERVES **4**   PREP AND COOKING TIME **30 minutes, plus up to 3 hours for marinating**

2 8-oz. packages of tempeh or homemade tempeh (page 198), cut into 4-in.-long and 2- to 3-in.-thick slices

MARINADE

1 thumb-size piece of fresh ginger, peeled and minced
2 garlic gloves, chopped
   A pinch of red pepper flakes
1 tsp. miso paste
   Grated zest and juice of 1 orange

2 tbsps. sesame oil
1 tbsp. olive oil
¼ cup amino acids, preferably Bragg's

TORTILLAS

½ cup black sesame seeds, crushed with fingers
2 cups masa harina
1¼ cups hot water
¼ tsp. salt

FIXINGS

   Blueberry-Guinness BBQ Sauce (page 204) or your favorite BBQ sauce, heated
1 avocado, pitted, peeled, and sliced
   Cranberry-Almond Slaw (page 118)

SPECIAL EQUIPMENT

   BBQ grill (gas or charcoal)

(NO GRILL?)

If not using a grill, you can sear the tempeh in a 10-inch skillet set on medium-high. Add 1 tablespoon of canola oil to the pan and heat until shimmering. Working in batches, sear both sides of the tempeh, about 2 minutes per side.

MARINATE THE TEMPEH

1. Put all of the marinade ingredients in a blender and process until smooth.
2. Place the tempeh strips in 9 x 13-inch glass baking dish. With a silicone pastry brush, coat all sides of the tempeh with marinade. Cover the dish with plastic wrap and refrigerate for at least 30 minutes or up to 3 hours. Tempeh can get crumbly so don't marinate it for more than 3 hours.

MAKE THE TORTILLAS

1. While the tempeh is marinating, toast the sesame seeds in a small 6-inch skillet (preferably cast-iron) until fragrant, about 5 minutes. Remove from heat.
2. In a medium bowl, mix together masa harina, sesame seeds, and hot water until thoroughly combined. Turn dough onto a clean surface and knead until pliable and smooth. If dough is too sticky, add more masa harina; if too dry, sprinkle with water.

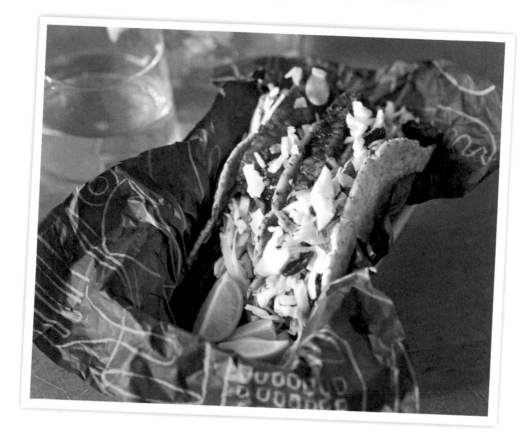

3. Preheat a 9-inch skillet or griddle (preferably cast-iron) on medium-high. Divide dough into 15 equal-size balls (about the size of a golf ball); make sure to dip your fingers in a bowl of water each time you form a ball.

4. Using a tortilla press, a rolling pin, or your hands, press each ball of dough flat between two sheets of plastic wrap until tortilla is $1/16$ inch thick and about 9 inches in diameter.

5. Working quickly, place each tortilla in preheated pan and allow to cook for approximately 30 seconds, or until browned and slightly puffy. Turn tortilla over to brown on second side for approximately 30 seconds more, then transfer to a plate. Repeat process with each ball of dough. Keep tortillas covered with a towel to stay warm and moist as you grill the tempeh.

GRILL THE TEMPEH

1. Fire up the grill to medium-high (see Note).

2. Grill the marinated tempeh on both sides until nice and charred, about 2 minutes per side. Toss the seared tempeh in the heated BBQ sauce.

SERVE

Serve in a tortilla, topped with avocado and slaw.

HEAVENLY
LEEKY SHIITAKE GRAVY-N-BISCUITS $$$

Why do the majority of restaurants turn out a bland, boring vegan version of this famed US-of-A classic? Rejoice, because now you no longer have to suffer the subpar embarrassment served at many dining establishments. You can make an infinitely superior version of this dish right in your own kitchen. This stuff is good, and it's versatile: after you get the hang of this basic recipe, you can flip it in many different ways—for brunch, dinner, or whatever, depending on what you pair it with.

SERVES **5**   PREP AND COOKING TIME **1 ½ hours**

GRAVY

- 3 tbsps. vegetable shortening, or Earth Balance Natural Buttery Spread
- 1 leek, white and light green parts sliced in half lengthwise and julienned, cleaned
- 2 garlic cloves, minced
- 1 tsp. minced fresh sage
- 12 oz. vegan chorizo, preferably Melissa's Soyrizo
- 1 lb. shiitake mushrooms, cleaned and sliced

SOUR SOY MILK

To make sour soy milk, add 1 tablespoon apple cider vinegar to 1 cup soy milk and let the mixture sit until curdled, about 5 minutes.

- ¼ cup all-purpose flour
- ½ tsp. sea salt
- ¼ tsp. freshly ground black pepper
- 2 cups coconut milk
- 1 cup soy milk
- 3 tsps. veggie bouillon, preferably Superior Touch
- 1 tsp. amino acids, preferably Bragg's

BISCUITS

- 2 ½ cups Self-Rising Flour (page 192), plus some to flour the board
- 3 tbsps. nonhydrogenated vegetable shortening
- 6 tbsps. Earth Balance Natural Buttery Spread, frozen
- ¾ cup sour soy milk (see Note)

TOPPINGS

- 10 cherry tomatoes, halved
  Crispy leeks (page 66)

MAKE THE GRAVY

1. In a 12-inch, heavy-bottomed skillet (preferably cast-iron) set on medium, heat the shortening or Earth Balance until shimmering. Add the leeks and sauté until soft, about 5 minutes. Add the garlic and sage and sauté for 3 minutes more. Increase the heat to medium-high and add the soyrizo, breaking it up with a spatula. Stir in the mushrooms and sauté until the sausage is browned, about 5 minutes. Add the flour, salt, and pepper, stirring constantly until flour begins to brown, about 5 minutes.
2. Slowly pour in the coconut milk and soy milk, stirring constantly and letting the mixture come to a boil. Add the bouillon and aminos, and reduce heat to low. Cook for 5 minutes, stirring occasionally. The gravy will thicken as it cools, so if you want thinner gravy, add a little more coconut milk. Keep it warm while you make the biscuits.

MAKE THE BISCUITS

1. Preheat oven to 425°F.
2. In a medium bowl, add the shortening to the self-rising flour, using your hands to quickly combine.
3. With a box grater, grate the Earth Balance into the flour-shortening mixture and toss with a fork.
4. Form a well in the center of the flour and pour in the soy milk. Toss with a fork until a thick dough forms.
5. Turn dough out onto a floured board, counter top, or piece of parchment. Gently knead the dough 2 or 3 times and roll or pat it into a ½-inch-thick rectangle or round. If the dough is too sticky, sprinkle a little flour on top. If it's too dry, add a little more soy milk.
6. With a floured 2-inch biscuit cutter, cut out your biscuits. Gently scrunch the scraps into a mound and cut more biscuits. These are the "scrap" biscuits: they will not be as tender as the first biscuits you cut, but they are still the bomb.
7. Place the unbaked biscuits ½ inch apart on an ungreased baking sheet. Bake until golden brown, 12 to 20 minutes.

SERVE

To serve the biscuits and gravy, cut the biscuits in half and place 4 halves on each plate. Pour the gravy over the biscuits and top with the halved cherry tomatoes and crispy leeks, or your favorite grilled veggies.

DANTE FRIED CHICKEN

MARCH 22
6PM–1PM
SANTOS PARTY HOUSE / $6

Eco Fresh Yo! Earth Day!
Veggie Cook UP & BBQ
with special guests

April 2

RISE UP!

UNITE AGAINST BIG CHICKEN!

DANTE FRIED CHICKEN
FAMILY BBQ
K.F.C.R.I.P. IN THE PARK

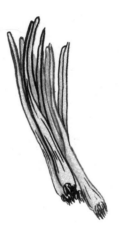

This chapter celebrates the sidekicks, the veggie and vegan recipes that heighten the experience of the main dish. My sides have crazy-huge personality delivered in banging little portions.

The back story: between 1995 and 2001, I was a pescatarian; I wanted to experiment with not eating meat. I have to admit that was the healthiest I ever felt. I used to fiend for my grandmother's food, though, and that was the challenge: how to compensate for the missing flavor from the bacon grease and the ham hock in the veggies. So I worked hard to develop flavorful vegan dishes, and I love the way they turned out. People still ask if there's pork in the collard greens! It took me a while to build the confidence to cook with ingredients that weren't mad prevalent in my childhood, but I got there eventually. This chapter has a lot of tips and tricks that will help you get comfortable with veggie cooking (if you're not already).

SWEDEN, ALL DAY EVERYDAY

One of my most memorable trips ever was when I went to Sweden with my buddies Rye Rye and Leif. I ended up at a friend's crazy, Burning Man–type arts festival in Gagnoff, the northern most point of Sweden. Apparently it started as someone's birthday party and grew into an artist cooperative *happening* over the years. It was really cool: everyone goes up the week prior to build tree houses and clubs; they even built me a portable kitchen and set up an oil-drum BBQ pit smoker. We were partying so damn hard and the sun never went down, which made the whole thing kind of dreamlike. Don't get it twisted—it was very grimy—but at the same time, mad fun.

Swedes lining up for famous DFC home cooking. *Skål!*

ENDIVES (WITH) HOPPIN' JOHN HUMMUS

This dish is very special to me because it was my first-ever DFC appetizer, created for my debut catering job. It's an instant classic and really easy to make. I love the earthy smokiness of the black-eyed peas—they give garbanzo beans a run for their money—plus, they're awesome combined with the freshness of the endive. My homies in Sweden especially love this dish; I make a ton of it for those guys. To me, hummus is best with loads of tahini, so there's a lot of it here.

MAKES **15 pieces**   PREP AND COOKING TIME **30 minutes**

15 endive leaves, washed
   and dried

HUMMUS
1 16-oz. can of black-eyed peas,
   rinsed and drained
3 to 6 tbsps. tahini

2 garlic cloves, smashed
½ tsp. sea salt
2 tbsps. olive oil
1 tsp. ground cumin
1 tsp. white pepper
3 tbsps. fresh lemon juice
¼ cup Veggie Stock (page 194)

TOPPING
1 squirt of amino acids,
   preferably Bragg's
1 roasted red or yellow bell pepper,
   finely diced
1 shallot, minced
½ cup minced fresh parsley
½ cup crumbled feta cheese

MAKE THE HUMMUS
In a blender, combine the black-eyed peas, tahini, garlic, salt, olive oil, cumin, white pepper, lemon juice, and stock. Mix on low until smooth, about 3 minutes, stopping several times to scrape down the sides of blender with a spatula.

MAKE THE TOPPING
In a small bowl, combine the amino acids, pepper, shallots, and parsley.

SERVE
Using a butter knife or small spatula, fill each endive leaf with 1 tablespoon of hummus. Top each filled endive with some pepper mixture and crumbled feta.

NOISETTES' GARLIC STRING BEANS

Heads up: these are not those mushy string beans you get at average soul food restaurants. Forget beans from a can or any of that frozen yuck. No chance—these beans are firm and flavorful all the way. Other than the flavor factor, I like this dish because it's so simple—believe it or not, I do appreciate simplicity in food! This culture-smashing recipe has a good mix of the Chinese and Korean sauce combinations that everyone in my family loved. Serve it as an entrée with some beans and rice or as a side dish at your celebrations.

SERVES **4 to 6**   PREP AND COOKING TIME **35 minutes**

2 tsps. olive oil
5 garlic cloves, minced or pressed
6 basil leaves, minced
1 lb. green beans, trimmed and
   cut into 2-in. pieces

1 carrot, grated
1 turnip, peeled and grated
6 cherry tomatoes, halved
2 tbsps. amino acids,
   preferably Bragg's

1 cup water
½ tsp. tomato paste
   Freshly ground black pepper
   Toasted sesame oil

Dante cooking up with Shingai Shoniwa from the the Noisettes.

1. In a 12-inch nonstick skillet set on medium, heat the oil until shimmering. Add the garlic and basil, then sauté until the edges of the garlic start to brown, about 3 minutes. Add the beans, carrot, and turnip, and sauté for 5 minutes.
2. Add the tomatoes and aminos.
3. Add the water, and stir in the tomato paste. Cover and cook until beans are bright green and still crisp, about 2 minutes. Season with pepper to taste.
4. Remove cover, increase heat to high, and cook until most of the water has evaporated, stirring frequently, until beans are crisp-tender, lightly browned, and beginning to wrinkle, 1 to 3 minutes longer.
5. When beans reach the desired tenderness, drizzle with toasted sesame oil. Serve immediately..

CORN -N- GINGER MAC SALAD

Usually I wouldn't touch macaroni salad with a ten-foot pole, but this dish is not the ubiquitous bland, no-love-just-mayo-salt-and-sugar concoction you're used to. This one is flipped with Indian spices. And guess what? You can easily go vegan on it if you'd like; just use eggless mayonnaise for the mayo in place of the mayo and sour cream and skip the Parmesan. Vegan or not, you're gonna love it.

SERVES **4 to 6**   PREP AND COOKING TIME **30 to 40 minutes**

1   tsp. ground cardamom
1   tsp. freshly grated nutmeg
3   tbsps. sour cream
1   cup coconut milk
½   cup mayonnaise or eggless mayonnaise, preferably Spectrum Light Canola Mayo
¾   tsp. dry mustard
1½ tsps. white sugar or agave nectar
1½ tbsps. apple cider vinegar, preferably Bragg's

½   tsp. sea salt, plus more to taste
2   cups elbow macaroni, cooked until tender, drained, and rinsed
⅓   cup diced celery
1   small red bell pepper, ribs and seeds removed, diced
3   tbsps. pistachios, toasted and finely crushed
1   tbsp. golden raisins or dried cranberries

2   green onions, minced
¼   cup minced red onion, soaked in cold water for 5 minutes and drained
2   tbsps. minced fresh parsley or cilantro
½   cup diced vine-ripened or heirloom tomatoes
½   cup grated Parmesan Freshly ground black pepper

1. In a 4-quart sauce pan set on medium, toast the cardamom and nutmeg until fragrant, about 5 minutes. Add the sour cream and the coconut milk to toasted spices. Reduce to low and simmer for 20 minutes. Remove from heat and cool completely.
2. In a medium bowl, whisk together the spiced coconut-cream mixture, mayonnaise, mustard, sugar or agave, cider vinegar, and ½ teaspoon salt. If the dressing is too thick, add more coconut milk to thin the consistency.
3. In a large bowl, combine the cooked macaroni, celery, bell pepper, nuts, raisins or cranberries, green onion, red onion, parsley or cilantro, tomato, and Parmesan.
4. Pour dressing over the mac and veg, and stir to combine. Season with salt and pepper to taste. The salad will keep in the refrigerator, covered in an airtight container, for up to 2 days.

DIRTY CURRY BEANS-N-RICE

Red beans and rice is a Cajun staple simmered in bean stock with an (un)healthy dose of animal fats. Rice and peas is a Caribbean mainstay cooked in coconut milk. I like both dishes, so you know what I did? I took the best of both worlds and joined them, without the animal fats. The result is a bang-up, flavor-rich taste of two cultures.

SERVES **6 to 8**   PREP AND COOKING TIME **45 minutes**

2 tsps. paprika
1 tbsp. curry powder
1 tsp. cumin seeds
½ tsp. dried sage
1 tsp. red pepper flakes
2 bay leaves
2 tbsps. canola oil
1 yellow onion, chopped
1 red bell pepper, ribs and
    seeds removed, chopped

2 celery stalks, chopped
3 garlic cloves, minced
1 tsp. grated fresh ginger
2 cups (uncooked) long grain rice
1½ tbsps. soy sauce
1 cup water
1 cup Veggie Stock (page 194)
2 cups coconut milk

1 15-oz. can of kidney beans,
    drained and rinsed
2 tsps. dried thyme
1 whole Scotch bonnet chili
    (or any hot chili)
    Freshly grated nutmeg (optional)
    Juice of ½ a lime (optional)

RICE COOKER

If you are not a black belt in stove-top rice cooking (as I, admittedly, am not), follow the procedure through step 5 and then throw everything into a rice cooker. Keep in mind that all rice cookers are not created equal. Some rice cookers (the less expensive kind, usually) may burn your rice because of all the additional ingredients, especially the coconut milk.

TOAST THE SPICES

Heat a 6-inch sauté pan on medium until hot. Add all the dry spices and the bay leaves to pan and gently toast, stirring frequently, until fragrant and just beginning to smoke, about 2 minutes. Transfer toasted spice mix to a small bowl and set aside.

MAKE THE BEANS AND RICE

1. In a 6-quart stock pot set on medium-high, heat the canola oil until shimmering. Add the onion, bell pepper, and celery, and sauté until vegetables begin to brown on the edges, about 6 to 8 minutes.
2. Add the garlic, ginger, toasted spices, and rice, stir well. Cook, stirring frequently, for another 2 to 3 minutes.

EXTRA VEGGIE
UMAMI

There are a lot of tricks you can do to add non-meaty, awesome savoriness (or umami, as the Japanese coined it) to veggie dishes, adding extra flavor without using animal fats and keeping the food 100% certified vegan. Take dried beans—if you cook them with spices, onion, celery, and garlic in olive oil, the flavors will penetrate the beans before you've even started boiling them up in stock. Caramelizing certain vegetables will do this too, such as charring tomatillos for collard greens. The sweetness and slightly burnt sugars impart deeper flavors into any dish. Deepening flavor is often as simple as oven roasting and pre-seasoning some of the ingredients you use in a recipe.

3. Add the soy sauce, water, stock, and coconut milk. Stir well.
4. Add the kidney beans and sprinkle in the thyme, stirring to combine.
5. Toss in Scotch bonnet chili and a little nutmeg. No need to mix. You just want the essence of these flavors. Don't worry about the hot pepper bringing the heat on; it will season the rice much like a bay loaf would (see Note).
6. Cover and simmer beans and rice on low for 15 minutes, and check for doneness. Do NOT stir. Continue cooking until rice is tender, about 5 minutes more.
7. When rice is cooked, remove pot from heat and let sit, covered, for 10 minutes. Discard the chili. Fluff rice and beans with a fork and sprinkle with some lime juice, if you want, before serving.

CRANBERRY- ALMOND SLAW

I just can't get with any store-bought, cabbage slop slaw, so I'm here to change all that by revisiting the way a slaw base is usually made. This is a totally familiar, yet ninja, slaw experience that is lighter, fresher, and punchier than the norm. We start with a simmered coconut milk–and-leek sauce, then mix in toasted almonds, dried cranberries, and a touch of maple syrup. *Boom!* You've got yourself an all-new slaw. One bite and you'll never do pre-prepped slaw again. You can make this slaw vegan by replacing the dairy with your favorite tofu alternative.

SERVES **6 to 8**   PREP AND COOKING TIME **45 minutes**

SLAW
- 1 medium cabbage head, shredded (about 5 cups)
- 1 small red cabbage head, shredded (about 3 cups)
- 1 cup sliced almonds, toasted
- 2 cups dried cranberries
- 2 celery stalks, diced
- ¼ cup chopped chives
- ½ medium red onion, diced
- 1 large carrot or 2 small carrots, shredded

DRESSING
- 1 tbsp. olive oil
- 1 leek, cleaned and white and light green parts julienned
- 1 garlic clove, chopped
- 1 tsp. apple cider vinegar, preferably Bragg's

- 1 cup coconut milk (you may need a little more)
- 2 tbsps. pure maple syrup
- ½ tsp. veggie bouillon
  Dash celery seed, or to taste
- 1 tbsp. mayonnaise
- ½ cup Mexican crema or sour cream
  Sea salt and freshly ground black pepper

MAKE THE SLAW
In a large plastic bowl with a snap-on lid, combine the cabbage, almonds, cranberries, celery, chives, onion, and carrots. Cover and refrigerate until ready to serve.

MAKE THE DRESSING
1. In 10-inch pan set on medium, heat the oil until shimmering. Toss in the leeks and sauté until they soften, about 4 minutes. Add the garlic and sauté for 1 minute more. Add the vinegar, coconut milk, maple syrup, and veggie bouillon, then simmer the mixture for another 5 minutes. Stir in the celery seed, transfer to a bowl, and cool completely.
2. In a blender, purée cooled dressing until smooth, and return it to the bowl. Add the mayonnaise and crema or sour cream, stirring to combine. If the dressing is too thick, add more coconut milk. Season with salt and pepper to taste, then cover and refrigerate for 30 minutes.

SERVE
Just before serving, pour the dressing over the slaw and stir well.

//SPANISH// BLACK-✺'D PEAS

Originally cultivated in Africa and Asia and brought to the southern United States in the 1700s, black-eyed peas are a cornerstone of Transatlantic African cuisine. They're also known as field pigeon peas, cow peas, and *frijoles de carita*. Whatever you call them, this was mostly a holiday dish for my family, cooked up on MLK Day and on New Year's, when they're supposed to bring you good luck. But really, you can eat them anytime. For this recipe, I throw a curve ball by adding yams or sweet potatoes and simmering the beans in a Mexican-influenced broth fortified with roasted garlic and poblano peppers.

SERVES **6 to 8**   PREP AND COOKING TIME **1 ½ to 2 ½ hours, or until tender**

2 poblano peppers, ribs and seeds removed, chopped
3 garlic cloves, minced
3 tbsps. olive oil
1 tbsp. water or beer
1 medium yellow onion, diced
2 celery stalks, diced
1 tsp. smoked paprika
2 tbsps. DFC Meat Rub (page 191) or chili powder
1 tsp. ground cumin
2 bay leaves

A pinch of dried sage
A pinch of dried rosemary
A pinch of dried basil
1 tbsp. creamy peanut butter
1 lb. dry (see Note) or frozen black-eyed peas
5 to 8 cups water or Chicken or Veggie Stock (pages 194–195)
3 medium yams or sweet potatoes, peeled and cut into chunks

1 red bell pepper, ribs and seeds removed, diced
1 jalapeño, ribs and seeds removed, chopped
2½ cups smoked tofu or any smoked meat, cubed (optional)
2 tbsps. amino acids, preferably Bragg's
   Freshly ground black pepper

1. Preheat oven to 375°F.
2. In a 2-quart ovenproof dish, toss the poblano pepper and ²/₃ of the garlic with 2 tablespoons of the olive oil. Roast for 15 minutes, or until the peppers become a little charred. Remove from oven and let cool.
3. In a blender, liquefy the roasted poblanos and garlic with a tablespoon or so of water or beer. Set aside.
4. In an 8-quart stock pot or Dutch oven set on medium, add the remaining olive oil and heat until shimmering. Add the onion and celery and sauté until translucent, about 5 minutes.
5. Add the remaining garlic, all of the spices (except the black pepper), and the peanut butter. The consistency should be a moist paste. If the mixture becomes too dry, add some water.

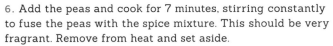

NOTE ABOUT DRY PEAS

If you're using dry peas, pre-soak them overnight in water that covers the peas by 3 inches. Drain and rinse before cooking.

6. Add the peas and cook for 7 minutes, stirring constantly to fuse the peas with the spice mixture. This should be very fragrant. Remove from heat and set aside.

7. Add enough water or stock to fill a stock pot three-quarters full. Toss in the yams or sweet potatoes, bell pepper, jalapeño, and, if using, the smoked tofu or smoked meat. Stir in the poblano mixture and season with aminos and black pepper to taste.

8. Bring the mixture to a boil. Reduce heat to low, cover pot, and simmer for 1½ hours, or, if using dry peas, until the peas are tender. If using frozen peas, simmer until the yams are tender. The consistency should be that of a thin gravy. Add more water or stock during simmering, if necessary.

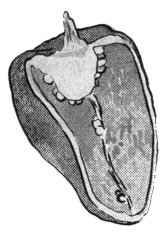

CREAMED SPINACH·N·ASPARAGUS

OOOH, I loved my grandmother's creamed spinach growing up, but it's way too rich for me now. That doesn't stop me from making it, though; I just had to slow its roll by coming up with a lighter incarnation. (I'm guessing you'd like to know her version, so here it is: fry bacon until crispy, drain, and then crumble it. Sauté the spinach in the bacon grease and add shallots, spices, cream, asparagus, and top with Parmesan.) I flip it by using coconut milk and peanut oil and roasting the asparagus—no bacon required.

SERVES **6**   PREP AND COOKING TIME **45 minutes**

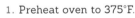

1   lb. asparagus, tough
    ends removed
1   lbsp. peanut oil or canola oil
    Sea salt and freshly ground
    black pepper
3   lbs. fresh spinach,
    tough stems removed

2   to 3 tbsps. unsalted butter,
    or 3 slices bacon
½   cup finely chopped
    shallots (optional)
1   tsp. minced garlic
1   cup thick coconut milk or
    heavy cream

¼   tsp. freshly grated nutmeg
¼   tsp. toasted curry powder
½   lb. fresh baby mozzarella,
    halved (optional)
    Shaved Parmesan,
    for garnish (optional)
12 cherry tomatoes, halved,
    for garnish (optional)

1. Preheat oven to 375°F.
2. In a medium bowl, lightly coat the asparagus with the olive or peanut oil, salt, and pepper. Transfer asparagus to a baking sheet and roast until browned, 15 to 20 minutes. Cool, then chop asparagus into bite-size pieces.
3. Bring a large pot of salted water to boil. Add the spinach and cook for 2 minutes. Drain through a fine-mesh strainer, pressing spinach with a large spoon to release as much water as possible. Finely chop drained spinach and set aside.
4. In a 10-inch sauté pan set on medium-high, melt the butter or oil. (Or fry the bacon if using for fat. Crumble bacon and reserve.) Add the shallots and garlic, and cook, stirring occasionally, until soft and fragrant, about 2 minutes.
5. Add the spinach and asparagus, and cook, stirring frequently, just until the liquid is evaporated, about 3 minutes. Add the cream, nutmeg, and curry powder and cook until cream has reduced by half. If using the mozzarella, toss it in now and cook for 1 minute, stirring to combine. Season with salt and pepper. Remove from the heat and serve it up garnished with shaved Parmesan, the crumbled bacon, and cherry tomatoes, if you like.

TOMATILLO COLLARDS

I love tomatillos—the tangy fruit goes well with everything from gumbo to rice and beans—and I've discovered it's the perfect complement to collard greens. It all started when I learned how to make Turkish-style collard greens from a Turkish friend from Seattle. When I took a taste, I knew immediately that the greens would pop if I adapted the original dish by mixing it with my tomatillo recipe. Warning to all you collard-green nonbelievers out there: we just hooked your tongue up!

SERVES **6 to 8**   PREP AND COOKING TIME **1 ½ hours**

- 2 cups white vinegar
- 3 large bunches collard greens
- 2 bunches kale
- 2 medium tomatillos, paper shell removed, chopped
- 5 garlic cloves, coarsely chopped
- 3 tbsps. olive oil
- 2 leeks, thoroughly rinsed, white and light green parts thinly sliced
- 1 small yellow onion, diced
- 2 celery stalks, diced

- 2 tbsps. minced fresh parsley
- 1 bay leaf
- 1 red bell pepper, ribs and seeds removed, diced
- 2 tbsps. amino acids, preferably Bragg's
- 8 cups water
- 2 tbsps. veggie bouillon
- 2 tsps. Sriracha
- 2 to 4 tbsps. turbinado sugar (raw sugar)

- 1 jalapeño, red or green, ribs and seeds removed, diced
- 2 tbsps. apple cider vinegar, preferably Bragg's
- 2 sweet potatoes, peeled and diced
- 1 pint cherry tomatoes, whole
- 8 oz. smoked tofu, cubed (optional) Sea salt and freshly ground black pepper

PREP THE GREENS

1. Fill a very clean sink or large stock pot halfway with cold water. Add the white vinegar and a few pinches of salt. Toss in the collard greens and kale. Let soak for 3 minutes. Drain.

2. Wash collards and kale a second time in plain water. Drain. If there is dirt at the bottom of sink or pot, rinse greens once more. Pat washed greens dry with paper towels.

3. Remove stems from collards and kale. Stack 6 to 8 leaves on top of one another, roll them up, and julienne. Set aside in a large bowl.

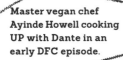

Master vegan chef Ayinde Howell cooking UP with Dante in an early DFC episode.

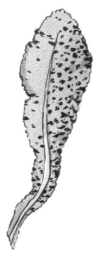

PREP THE TOMATILLOS

1. Preheat oven to 350°F.
2. In a small bowl, toss the tomatillos and garlic with 1 tablespoon olive oil. On a baking sheet, arrange tomatillos and garlic in a single layer, and roast for 20 to 25 minutes. Transfer roasted veg to a small bowl to cool.
3. In a blender, purée cooled tomatillos and garlic with a little water. Set aside.

COOK IT UP

1. In a 6-quart pot on medium, heat the 2 remaining tablespoons olive oil. Add the leeks, onion, celery, parsley, bay leaf, and bell pepper. Add some of the greens and kale to the pot, adding more as they cook down. Stir in aminos.
2. Add 8 cups water, veggie bouillon, Sriracha, sugar to taste, jalapeño, apple cider vinegar, and the tomatillo purée. Bring mixture to boil, then reduce to low.
3. Add the sweet potatoes and smoked tofu, if using. Cook on low for 45 minutes.
4. Stir in the cherry tomatoes, and continue cooking for 15 minutes, or until the greens are as tender as you like. Season with salt and pepper to taste.

FRESH! CORN-N-CUCUMBER SALAD

This was an all-time favorite summertime salad in my family, and it's a dish that people who refuse to eat veggies clamor for. It might sound boring on paper, but after you take your first bite you'll understand what the fuss is about. Super-fresh-tasting, it's especially good with fried or barbecued food, and it provides all the vegetables you need so you don't have to serve multiple, plain-Jane veggie sides. If you're down with meat, serve it up with crispy bacon. If not, top it with toasted sesame seeds or peanuts—that's how I like it. Oh, and heads up: the recipe doubles well for big parties.

SERVES **4 to 6**   PREP AND COOKING TIME **45 minutes**

VEGGIES

3 ears sweet corn, shucked
¼ lb. wax beans, chopped
¼ lb. snap peas, fibrous
   string removed
¼ lb. string beans, chopped
1 small broccoli head,
   stems removed
3 large cucumbers or two
   English cucumbers, peeled
   (if you like), seeded, and diced
8 cherry tomatoes, halved
1 small red onion, diced

2 radishes, diced
1 avocado, pitted and diced
1 large carrot, grated
1 small golden beet, peeled
   and grated
1 handful bean sprouts, rinsed

DRESSING

1 small piece of fresh ginger,
   peeled and chopped
4 tbsps. extra virgin olive oil
2 tbsps. sesame oil

¾ cup amino acids,
   preferably Bragg's
3 tbsps. apple cider vinegar,
   preferably Bragg's
1 tsp. fresh lemon juice
2 tbsps. yellow mustard
1 small garlic clove, minced
   Sea salt and freshly ground pepper
1 tbsp. fresh basil, mint, cilantro,
   or parsley, minced (optional)
   Toasted sesame seeds (optional)
   Crushed roasted peanuts (optional)

MAKE THE VEG

1. Bring a stock pot filled three-quarters with water to boil.
2. While water is heating, prepare an ice bath for the veggies.
3. Blanch the corn, wax beans, snap peas, string beans, and broccoli head for 3 minutes, then transfer veggies to ice bath for 2 minutes. Drain. Put beans and snap peas into a serving bowl.
4. Cut the corn kernels from the cobs and add them to the beans.
5. Separate the broccoli crown into small florets and add them to the bowl.
6. To the same bowl add the cucumbers, tomatoes, onion, radishes, avocado, carrot, beet, and bean sprouts.

MAKE THE DRESSING

Put the ginger, both oils, aminos, vinegar, lemon juice, mustard, and garlic in a blender, and purée until smooth. Season to taste with salt and pepper.

SERVE

Pour the dressing over vegetables, tossing to combine. Garnish the salad with your chosen herb and sesame seeds or crushed peanuts, if you get down like that. Eat the salad right away or refrigerate it for a few hours (but don't dress it until you serve).

DRUNK
SPANISH RICE

Mexican rice is the de facto sidekick of Mexican cuisine, along with tortilla and beans, and I grew up eating it on the regular. This dish, my take on the classic, pairs well with most everything in this book. I updated the game by substituting edamame for corn and lacing the dish with pale ale to give it a little more swagger. There are no shortcuts or fake ingredients in this recipe (as usual), and it's extra simple to make, so you wouldn't want (or need) to fake anything anyway.

SERVES 6   **PREP AND COOKING TIME 40 minutes**

2 tbsps. canola oil
1½ cups long-grain rice
1 small onion, finely diced
2 garlic cloves, minced
1 tsp. ground cumin
1 tbsp. chili powder
½ cup tomato sauce

2 cups Veggie Stock (page 194)
½ cup your favorite pale ale
2 tbsps. minced fresh parsley
½ to 1 cup frozen edamame, thawed
Sea salt
Freshly ground black pepper

1. In a 10-inch sauté pan set on medium-high, heat the oil until shimmering. Add the rice, stirring to coat. Cook for 5 minutes, stirring occasionally.
2. Add the onion, garlic, cumin, and chili powder, and sauté for 1 minute.
3. Add the tomato sauce, stock, beer, parsley, and edamame, stirring to combine. Increase heat to high and bring the rice to a boil.
4. Reduce heat to low, cover, and simmer the rice for 15 minutes. Do not lift the lid before the 15 minutes are up.
5. Turn off the heat, uncover the sauté pan, season with salt and pepper to taste, and fluff the rice with a fork. Re-cover the skillet and let it sit for up to 25 minutes before serving.

WTF! TOFU CHITTERLINGS

My connection to chitterlings (a dish made from pig intestines) runs deep: I cleaned out the intestines as a kid, helping out my grandmother in exchange for Transformers. It was really disgusting—I found glass, rocks, dirt, and random things up in there, and it all smelled like dead dragon ass. And people actually ate this stuff—WTF, right? But it was worth it: I was the only kid on the block to end up with damn near the whole collection of Transformers, even a bootleg Optimus Prime from Chinatown. Score! Anyway, I never thought I could reinvent the chitterlings my Grans served, but when I first had tofu skins (aka yuba) back in 1992, their texture reminded me of her heirloom offal classic! I don't eat chitterlings, but I was dying to experiment and see if I could come up with an alternative version of Grans' dish. And what do you know? I created a certified game-changer.

SERVES **6**   PREP AND COOKING TIME **2 ½ hours**

- 4 oz. dried tofu skins (yuba)
- 2 tbsps. peanut oil
- 1 small onion, diced
- 4 scallions, white and green parts, minced
- 1 orange bell pepper, ribs and seeds removed, chopped
- 1 jalapeño, ribs and seeds removed, diced

- 3 tomatillos, paper removed, chopped
- 3 garlic cloves
- 4 pieces fried bean curd, diced
- 1 15-oz. can hominy (drained)
- 4 cups Veggie Stock (page 194)
- 1 tbsp. amino acids, preferably Bragg's
- 1 tsp. vegetarian oyster sauce

- 6 oz. rice cake pasta
- ½ tsp. sesame oil
   Chopped fresh cilantro, for garnish
- 1 large tomato, chopped, for garnish

1. In a large bowl, soak the tofu skins in water for 2 hours, drain, and pat dry with paper towels. Cut the skins into 1-inch pieces.
2. In a 12-inch sauté pan set on medium, heat the peanut oil until shimmering. Add the onion, scallions, bell pepper, jalapeño, tomatillo, and garlic, sautéing until soft, about 8 minutes.
3. Add the tofu skins and fried bean curd and cook for 5 minutes. Toss in the hominy, stirring to combine.
4. Reduce the heat to low and pour in the stock, aminos, oyster sauce, rice cake pasta, and sesame oil. Simmer for 30 to 45 minutes. Garnish with cilantro and tomatoes.

DAC SUCCOTASH

Everybody loves this light, nutritious creation, finished with fresh tomato broth to loosen it up. Its delicious Malaysian influences reflect the legacy of that country's location on the spice route (see sidebar). Malaysia picked up a wide range of flavors from different parts of the world, represented here in this perfect balance of diverse ingredients: the sweetness from the corn and edamame make it pop, the okra gives it body, and the cracked black pepper lends a bit of heat. It's a super easy dish that's perfect served over rice.

SERVES 4 to 6   **PREP AND COOKING TIME 45 minutes**

OKRA
1 lb. okra, washed, and sliced into ½-inch pieces
2 tbsps. canola oil
   Sea salt and freshly ground black pepper

TOMATO BROTH
1 large tomato, chopped
   Leaves from 2 sprigs of Thai basil, chopped
1 heaping tbsp. vegetable bouillon
2 cups water

SUCCOTASH
1 tbsp. unsalted butter
2 tsps. toasted sesame oil
1 small red onion, diced
1 small orange bell pepper, ribs and seeds removed, diced
1 celery stalk, diced
1 thumb-sized piece of fresh ginger, peeled and minced
1 cup frozen edamame, thawed
2 cups fresh corn kernels
1 tbsp. amino acids, preferably Bragg's

MALAYSIA'S CULINARY COLLISION

Many cultural adaptations in history stem from the spice trade, which was born in the Middle Ages on the other side of the world. In its heyday, the spice trade was a global import-export business that fed the exchange of culinary traditions and practices. The history of the spice trade is prevalent in one of my favorite cuisines, Malaysian food. Because Malaysia was situated on the spice route, it was influenced by the cultures of native Malay, Chinese, Indian, and Thai societies. Malaysian food is similar to Creole in that it's a combination of diverse flavors and customs integrated into a big anthropological mix. Malaysian and Creole cooking styles are perfect examples of how different spices and techniques link Asia to Africa, and America to Europe. I consider Malaysian food a highlight of this celebration and marriage of regions.

Multi-talented designer/DJ Jon Santos in the kitchen with DFC, preppin' da Succotash!

ROAST THE OKRA

1. Preheat oven to 350°F.
2. In a large bowl, toss the okra with the oil and salt and pepper to taste.
3. Arrange okra in a single layer on a baking sheet and roast until slightly browned, about 15 minutes. Transfer to a bowl and set aside to cool.

MAKE THE TOMATO BROTH

1. In a 2-quart sauce pan, combine the tomato, basil, bouillon, and water. Bring to a boil, then reduce to low and simmer for 25 minutes.
2. Transfer the tomato broth to a blender (careful, it's hot!) and purée until smooth. Set aside.

MAKE THE SUCCOTASH

1. In a 4-quart sauté pan set on medium, heat the butter and toasted sesame oil. Add the onion, pepper, celery, and ginger, and sauté until translucent and aromatic, about 5 minutes.
2. Add the edamame, corn, roasted okra, and aminos, stirring to combine. Pour in a ½ cup of the tomato broth and stir. Add more broth as desired, and season with salt and pepper to taste. Cook on low for 10 minutes more. Serve over Drunk Spanish Rice (page 128).

ROOT UP! SLAW

This is my number-one favorite coleslaw recipe, inspired by fresh Asian salads rather than industrialized supermarket slaw. But don't worry—even though it's not traditional slaw, it still has a mad creaminess that comes from blending crushed toasted peanuts with coconut milk, peanut butter, and a touch of ginger. That's right—no dairy! This dish is seriously addictive—the mix of flavors hits the spot every damn time. It's a big winner with vegan eaters and those all up on a macrobiotic trip. It's so good, though, meat eaters beg for it too.

SERVES 4   PREP AND COOKING TIME **35 minutes**

1   medium cabbage head, shredded (about 5 cups)
1   small red cabbage head, shredded (about 3 cups)
2   red beets, peeled and shredded
1   cup peanuts, crushed (see Note)
½   cup minced celery
2   green onions, thinly sliced
1   leek, thoroughly washed, white and light green parts thinly sliced
½   red bell pepper, ribs and seeds removed, julienned

½   medium red onion, diced
2   dried sour plums, minced
¼   cup chopped fresh chives
1   fennel bulb, cored and julienned
1   large carrot, julienned
     A pinch celery seed, or to taste

DRESSING
1   tbsp. honey (optional)
¾   cup, or more, coconut milk
½   cup coconut water
2   tbsps. creamy peanut butter (see Note)
½   tsp. veggie bouillon

1   thumb-size piece of fresh ginger, peeled and finely chopped
1   garlic clove, minced
2   tbsps. amino acids, preferably Bragg's
     Toasted sesame oil
1   jalapeño, ribs and seeds removed, diced (optional)
     Freshly ground black pepper to taste
     Minced fresh cilantro to taste

ALLERGIC TO PEANUTS?

Try almonds instead of peanuts and almond butter instead of peanut butter.

SLAW THE VEG
Combine both cabbages, the beets, peanuts, celery, green onion, leek, bell pepper, and red onion in a large bowl with a snap-on lid. Cover and refrigerate until ready to serve.

MAKE THE DRESSING
In a blender, purée all dressing ingredients until smooth and creamy. The consistency should be like tahini. If it's too thick, add more coconut milk or coconut water. Transfer dressing to a bowl, cover, and refrigerate until ready to serve.

SERVE
Just before serving, pour the dressing over the slaw. Add black pepper and cilantro to taste. Stir well to combine.

COLLARD GREEN* ROLL UPZ

These roll upz make me think of dolmas, the stuffed grape leaves that I love, although I've always preferred the taste of collard green leaves. Start by prepping the leaves with a tasty ginger-sesame marinade and then once they're ready, load 'em up with whatever filling you'd like—a great one is Dirty Curry Beans-n-Rice served with some good ol' plum or peanut sauce. You could also fill 'em up with BBQ pork, grilled chicken, couscous and lamb, or braised tofu. Pick your fave and run with it.

MAKES **about two dozen**   PREP AND COOKING TIME **20 minutes to 1 hour, depending on the filling**

2 lbs. collard greens

MARINADE
¾ cup apple cider vinegar, preferably Bragg's
1 small onion, sliced
¼ cup amino acids, preferably Bragg's

1 garlic clove, minced
1 thumb-size piece of fresh ginger, peeled and minced
1 tsp. honey
1½ tbsps. toasted sesame oil
4 tbsps. olive oil
A pinch paprika

FILLING
Dirty Curry Beans-n-Rice (page 116), Drunk-n-Fruity Pulled Pork (page 90), or whatever filling you're feeling

MARINATE THE GREENS
1. Set up an ice bath for the collard greens.
2. Bring a large pot of water to boil; salt generously. Add the collard leaves in batches, blanching for 2 minutes. Transfer greens to the ice bath, and let them sit for 1 minute. Drain, and pat greens dry with paper towels..
3. With a sharp knife, remove the thickest part of the collards' stem, being careful to leave the leaf intact.
4. In a blender, purée all the marinade ingredients. Transfer to a small bowl.
5. On a cutting board, carefully spread out as many collard leaves as space will allow.

6. Dip a pastry brush into the marinade and coat both sides of each leaf, being careful not to tear them. Repeat with all collard leaves.

7. Wrap now or later. The longer the leaves marinate, the better. They will keep in a Ziploc bag or lidded Tupperware container for up to 3 days.

WRAP 'EM UP

1. When you're ready to wrap, lay leaves on a cutting board, rib side down, as you did when you brushed on the marinade. Gently overlap one side of each leaf on the other.

2. Spoon 1 tablespoon of filling onto the top center of leaf. Fold sides over filling. Roll it up, working away from you.

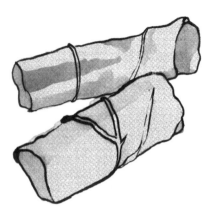

YUCCA MALUCA SPINACH STEW

I made this dish with NYC's Dominican It Girl and recording artist Maluca. Straight off, I could tell that she can really cook, which (let's face it) is majorly attractive. We had a blast together at the Red Bull Mad Decent party at London's Notting Hill Carnival and even made a DFC Show episode featuring our escapades. In Maluca's native Dominican Republic (and all of Latin America, for that matter) beans are a serious sport—you'll get dissed in a minute if you mess them up, so I had to be careful with this one. I could see that Maluca was initially skeptical of the strange ingredients I was throwing into the pot, and to top it off, I served them with Cranberry-Almond Rice. WTF?! But no worries, she flipped her wig over this stew.

SERVES **6 to 8**   PREP AND COOKING TIME **2 hours**

POBLANO PURÉE

- 1 poblano pepper, ribs and seeds removed, chopped
- 1 tomatillo, paper shell removed, chopped
- 5 garlic cloves, 2 peeled and 3 minced
- 2 tbsps. canola oil
- 12 oz. light-colored beer, such as pilsner

STEW

- 1 small yellow onion, diced
- 1 jalapeño pepper, ribs and seeds removed, diced
- 1 tsp. dried oregano
- 2 small yucca, peeled, cored, and diced
- 2 carrots, diced
- 1 celery stalk, diced
- 1 lb. dried red beans

- 1 tsp. creamy peanut butter
- 1 tsp. ground cumin
- 1 tbsp. chili powder
- 1 bay leaf
- 3 tsps. veggie bouillon
- 3 cups baby spinach, thoroughly washed
   Sea salt and freshly ground black pepper
- 2 tbsps. chopped fresh cilantro

MAKE THE POBLANO PURÉE

1. Preheat oven to 375°F.
2. In a small baking dish, combine the poblano, tomatillo, and 2 whole garlic cloves. Toss with 1 tablespoon oil and roast until slightly blackened, about 10 minutes.
3. Transfer roasted mixture to a blender and add the beer. Purée until smooth and set aside.

NYC Dominican It Girl, and chef in her own right, Maluca, making flavor history at the Mad Decent Notting Hill party with DFC.

MAKE THE STEW

1. In a 6-quart pot set on medium, heat remaining tablespoon oil until shimmering. Add the onion and jalapeño, and sauté until soft, about 5 minutes. Add the minced garlic and oregano and sauté 2 minutes more. Add the yucca, carrots, celery, beans, peanut butter, cumin, chili powder, and bay leaf, and sauté 2 to 4 minutes.

2. Stir in the poblano purée and the bouillon, then fill pot with enough water to cover the beans and veg by 2 inches. Bring to a boil, then reduce the heat to low. Simmer for 1 hour until the beans are soft. Smash some of the beans on the side of the pan to vary the texture.

3. Add the spinach and simmer for 20 minutes. Adjust seasoning with salt and pepper.

SERVE

Sprinkle the cilantro over top, and serve with Cranberry-Almond Rice (page 144).

NEW-SCHOOL ELOTE

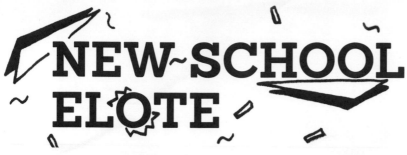

Elote is grilled corn on the cob covered with mayo, cheese, lime, and chili powder or paprika. I was scared to tamper with such a quintessential Mexican street food—Angelenos like their corn just the way it is. But I gave it the DFC treatment, and it quickly became the most-ordered menu item on the truck—people ate it up like crazy. I'm glad you approve, LA, you know I be reppin' da elote. Want the vegan version? Use eggless mayo and swap out the cheese for nutritional yeast like a lot of my customers did.

SERVES **4**   PREP AND COOKING TIME **20 minutes**

¼ cup mayonnaise
2 tbsps. honey, preferably raw
1 garlic clove, minced
½ cup toasted coconut flakes
1 tsp. crushed red pepper flakes

½ cup grated Parmesan cheese
4 ears of corn, husks peeled back and silk removed; the husks are the "handle"

4 tbsps. unsalted butter, melted
Chili powder, to taste

1. Preheat an outdoor grill (gas or charcoal) to medium-high heat.
2. In a shallow dish, whisk the mayo, honey, and garlic until smooth.
3. In another shallow dish, combine the toasted coconut, pepper flakes, and Parmesan.
4. Place the shucked corn directly on the preheated grill and cook, rotating the corn and keeping the husks away from the flames, until lightly charred all over, 7 to 10 minutes.
5. Roll the grilled corn in melted butter, then, using a pastry brush, coat them with the mayo mixture. Sprinkle with Parmesan mixture and garnish with chili powder. Serve immediately.

BLACK-N-GREEN DRAGON ROLLS

These rolls were easy to dream up, and so good I'm surprised I didn't think of it sooner. They came together when I had leftover collard greens from a party and spring roll wraps in the freezer. I decided to add a bunch of tasty ingredients to the collards, roll them up in the wraps, and BOOM—it was the Asia-to-Africa connection right there in my kitchen. Dip these in Hotty Totty Spicy Mustard, and you've got yourself a smart and tasty way to sneak some veggies into your life.

MAKES **2 to 3 dozen, depending on the size of the wrapper you choose** PREP AND COOKING TIME **1½ hours**

2 cups white vinegar
Salt
2 large bunches of collard greens, shredded
4 baby bok choy, chopped
2 tbsps. olive oil
1 tbsp. toasted sesame oil
1 leek, thoroughly washed, white and light green parts sliced
1 small onion, minced
1 celery stalk, diced
5 garlic cloves, minced
2 tbsps. chopped fresh parsley

1 dried bay leaf
2 tbsps. amino acids, preferably Bragg's
2 tbsps. veggie bouillon
1 tsp. miso paste
2 tsps. Sriracha
3 tbsps. turbinado sugar
Freshly ground black pepper
1 jalapeño, red or green, ribs and seeds removed, minced
1 large yam, diced
2 tbsps. apple cider vinegar, preferably Bragg's

1 8-oz. can whole water chestnuts, drained and slivered
2 cups cooked black beans
1 large egg, beaten
1 cup crumbled smoked tofu (optional)
1 gallon high-smoke-point oil, such as peanut or canola
24 to 36 store-bought egg roll wrappers

SPECIAL EQUIPMENT
Candy thermometer

MAKE THE FILLING

1. Fill your very clean sink or a large stock pot halfway with water, and add the vinegar and a palm full of salt. Toss in the collard greens and wash them thoroughly. Wash the greens a second time in plain water, if they need it. Pat dry the collards with paper towels.

2. Remove the stems from the collard greens. Stack 6 to 8 leaves, roll them up, and julienne the collards. Chop the strips into small pieces. Set the chopped collards aside in a large bowl.

3. Cut the baby bok choy in half and wash them thoroughly with water. Then place them cut side down and cut them into horizontal strips. Add them to the collards.

4. In a 6-quart heavy-bottomed pot set on medium-high, heat the olive oil and sesame oil until shimmering. Add the leek, onion, celery, garlic, parsley, and bay leaf. Gradually add the greens and bok choy. Cook them down, and add more until all the greens have been incorporated. Add aminos, stirring to combine.

5. Add the veggie bouillon, miso paste, Sriracha, sugar, black pepper to taste, jalapeño, yam, apple cider vinegar, water chestnuts, and black beans. Pour in just enough water to cover the vegetables, about 4 to 6 cups. Bring to a boil. Reduce the heat to low and simmer for 45 minutes.

6. Drain the vegetables in a colander set over a large bowl to catch the liquids. (I love this stuff! Use it to boil rice, or drink it as a broth. It's mad good.) Squeeze out as much liquid as possible, and let the vegetables cool completely.

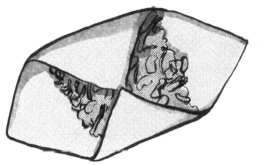 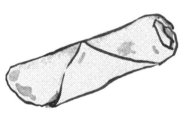

FILL AND FRY THE ROLLS

1. Prepare your deep fryer according to the instructions or fill a high-sided, heavy-bottomed Dutch oven or 12-inch skillet (preferably cast-iron) halfway with oil (about 3 inches) and heat to 350°F to 375°F (use a candy thermometer to take the oil temperature).

2. While oil heats, line a baking sheet with parchment. Lay a wrapper in front of you so that it forms a diamond shape. Use your index finger to wet all the edges with the beaten egg. Place 1 to 2 tablespoons of the filling near the point closest to you. Roll it away from you once, tuck in the sides, and then continue rolling. Seal the top point of the roll with a little more of the beaten egg and place the egg roll on the baking sheet. Repeat until all the wrappers are filled.

3. Working in batches of 3 or 4, fry the egg rolls until golden brown and crispy, about 3 minutes, turning halfway through. Using a slotted spoon, carefully remove the fried egg rolls from the oil and set them on paper towels or newspaper to drain. Serve warm with Hotty Totty Spicy Mustard (page 205).

$ANTIGOLD ~~SIGNATURE~~ MAC-N-CHEESE

I made this favorite recipe from my childhood on my web TV show with one of my favorite recording artists, Santigold. She's an awesomely humble person, and I felt so comfortable cooking alongside her. It was a special experience, even though she admitted to being dubious of how coconut, rosemary, and cheese would taste together. But if you watch the episode, you can see how excited she was when she tried it. It just goes to show that when good energy is in the kitchen, good things go into your mouth.

SERVES **6 to 8**   PREP AND COOKING TIME **45 minutes**

1 lb. elbow macaroni, or your favorite small pasta shape
   Olive oil
2 tbsps. unsalted butter
1 small red onion, minced
1 to 2 sprigs fresh rosemary, leaves minced

2 cups thick coconut milk
1 cup heavy cream
24 oz. cream cheese (1½ 16-ounce bricks)
2 cups grated Parmesan
1 garlic clove, minced (optional)
   A pinch cayenne pepper

   Sea salt and freshly ground pepper
6 cups grated sharp or extra sharp Cheddar
½ cup green onion, minced, or to taste
1 cup sweetened coconut flakes, preferably Baker's

1. With an oven rack positioned in upper third of oven, preheat oven to 375°F.
2. Cook the macaroni al dente, according to the directions on the package. Add a pinch of salt and a dab of olive oil to the boiling water.
3. When cooked, cool the mac by running it under cold water in a colander. Transfer to a bowl, toss with a little olive oil, and set aside.
4. In a 6-quart pot set on low, melt the butter. Add the red onion and rosemary, and sauté until fragrant and soft, about 5 minutes.
5. Add the coconut milk, cream, and cream cheese, and stir to combine. Simmer on low heat until cream cheese has melted, stirring constantly to avoid cheese sticking to the bottom of pan, about 5 minutes.

Dante cooking up with Santigold.

6. Add the Parmesan, garlic (if using), cayenne, and salt and pepper to taste, and stir until the cheese melts. Remove the sauce from the heat.

7. In a large bowl, combine the mac with the sauce, using a spatula to evenly coat the mac.

8. In a 9 x 13-inch baking dish, firmly pack half the cheesy mac, then cover it with a thin layer of Cheddar. Repeat process with other half of cheesy mac.

9. Top the mac and cheese with the remaining Cheddar, the green onion, and the coconut flakes.

10. Place baking dish on sheet pan and bake for 20 minutes, or until golden brown. Keep an eye on it because the coconut can burn pretty fast. Let cool at least 15 minutes before serving.

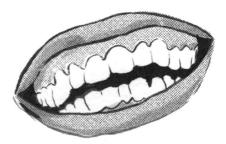

CRANBERRY-ALMOND RICE

This rice is another mainstay in the DFC repertoire. It's versatile and no-fuss but always gets strange gawks at first—cranberries at the supper table and it's not even Thanksgiving or Christmas? Cooking up dried fruit with rice is nothing new, though; they've been doing it in the Mediterranean for thousands of years. This rice has a mad aromatic, earthy taste, and the toasted almonds go well with the cranberries.

SERVES 8   PREP AND COOKING TIME 25 minutes

4 cups Veggie Stock (page 194)
½ tsp. turmeric
  A few strands of saffron
1 garlic clove, minced
⅛ tsp. chili powder
1 tsp. fresh lemon juice

2 cups aromatic rice
  (such as jasmine), uncooked
½ cup sliced almonds, toasted
½ cup dried cranberries
3 green onions, white and green
  parts chopped

1½ tbsps. amino acids,
  preferably Bragg's
¼ tsp. freshly ground black pepper,
  plus more to taste
1 tbsp. unsalted butter or olive oil

1. In a medium-size pot with a tight-fitting lid set on high, heat the stock.
2. While stock is coming to a boil, add the turmeric, saffron, garlic, chili powder, and lemon juice. Stir well. Pour in the rice, almonds, cranberries, green onion, and aminos. Stir again.
3. Once it boils, reduce heat to low and cover. Cook 12 to 15 minutes, or until all of the liquid has been absorbed by the rice. Do not lift the lid before the 12 to 15 minutes are up.
4. Turn off the heat and leave the pot, covered, on the burner for another 5 to 10 minutes, or until you're ready to serve. Just before serving, fluff the rice with a fork.

LOW COUNTRY SPECIAL OVER RICE

This dish is fairly easy to make, and it's a time-tested classic with three basic ingredients—sausage, beans, and rice. The classic is good, but you know I couldn't just sit on this without a good flip or two, so here you have it, DFC style. I added cut-up steak and okra to the mix, along with other choice elements. Roasting the okra gives the dish the right texture; we ain't down with the slime.

SERVES **6 to 8**   PREP AND COOKING TIME **3½ hours**

1 lb. dry kidney beans, rinsed and picked over
1 tbsp. canola oil
1 lb. beef stew meat, chopped
1 to 1½ lbs. Andouille or hot smoked sausage, sliced on the bias into bite-size pieces
1 large onion, chopped
1 red bell pepper, ribs and seeds removed, chopped

5 celery stalks, chopped
5 garlic cloves, minced
1 smoked ham hock (optional)
  A few dashes of amino acids, preferably Bragg's
  A few dashes of Sriracha or your favorite hot sauce
½ tsp. dried thyme
  A pinch cayenne pepper
1 tsp. chili powder

1 tsp. ground cumin (optional)
1 tbsp. DFC Fish Fry Mix (page 189)
1 dried bay leaf
1 tsp. cornstarch (omit if using okra)
1 whole jalapeño
6 to 8 cups Veggie Stock or Chicken Stock (pages 194–195)
½ lb. okra, tips removed, halved and roasted (optional)
  Sea salt and freshly ground pepper

PREP THE BEANS
Soak the kidney beans overnight in a large bowl. Rinse and keep the beans refrigerated until ready to use.

MAKE THE STEW
1. In a large heavy-bottomed pot or Dutch oven set on high, heat the oil until it begins to shimmer. Working in batches, sear the beef on all sides, about 3 minutes per batch. Transfer the seared meat to a medium bowl or shallow dish.
2. Add the sausage to the same pot and sauté until browned, about 5 minutes. Transfer the browned sausage to the bowl or dish with the seared beef. Reduce the heat to medium.

The first time I tasted Sriracha, I immediately knew that it was going to end up in many of my dishes. It's such an addictive blend of spices, sweetness, and heat, all without MSG! When I started researching Sriracha's heritage, not only did I find out that the legendary sauce has been brewed up by Huy Fong Foods in Los Angeles since 1980, but also that their goal was to become the Asian version of an all-encompassing, Heinz 57 type of sauce. What's cool is that Sriracha really has gone global. All chefs, from the guy running the 'hood fry shop down the block to Momofuku's David Chang get busy with Sriracha.

3. To the pot, add the onion, bell pepper, and celery, and sauté the vegetables until the onion is translucent, about 5 minutes. Add the garlic and sauté for 2 more minutes.

4. Stir in the beans, beef, sausage, ham hock, aminos, Sriracha, thyme, cayenne, chili powder, cumin, spice mix, bay leaf, cornstarch (if not using okra), and jalapeño.

5. Pour in the stock and bring to a boil, then reduce the heat to low. Simmer, stirring occasionally, for 1½ hours. Add the okra, if using, and simmer for 30 more minutes. The dish is done when the beans are soft and the stock becomes creamy, about 2 hours total. Season with salt and pepper to taste.

DOUBLE DUTCH TEMPEH-N-BEAN ♥CURD PATTIES♥

I'm on a quest to make sure all people can enjoy my food regardless of dietary preferences. So for the Santigold vs. Yo Majesty! *DFC Show* episode party, I came up with this banging veggie alternative to classic crab cakes. I had help from my homies at May Wah, who have some awesome, seafood-accented veggie proteins (that's the "faux salmon or tuna" in the recipe) that you can swap out for salmon, tuna, or crab. The final product is incredible—in fact, we once had a small scuffle at a party when a vegetarian accused a meat eater of overindulging. These are seriously that good.

SERVES **4 to 6**   PREP AND COOKING TIME **1½ hours**

PATTIES

3 tbsps. canola oil, plus more as needed

2 shallots, chopped

1 red bell pepper, ribs and seeds removed, finely diced

5 scallions, white and green parts finely chopped

1 lb. firm tofu, faux tuna, or faux salmon (see Note)

½ lb. Tempeh (page 198), ground

TOFU NOTE

If using tofu, place a plate on top of the prepackaged tofu with paper towels underneath to catch the water, and put weight on top of it (I use canned goods). Let stand at room temperature for 30 to 45 minutes. This will press out some of the excess liquid. Drain and pat dry. Break up the tofu into smaller pieces. If using faux fish, then just blitz it a little in your food processor or finely mince it.

1 tbsp. minced garlic

½ tsp. Chinese Five Spice powder

1½ tsps. Old Bay or DFC Fish Fry Spice Mix (page 189)

¼ tsp. white sugar

½ freshly ground white pepper

¼ to ½ cup eggless mayo, preferably Spectrum Light Canola mayo

3 tbsps. fresh lemon juice

¼ yellow or Dijon mustard

1 tsp. amino acids, preferably Bragg's

Seaweed flakes (omit if using faux tuna or salmon)

½ cup finely crushed Whole Foods vegan crackers

COATING

½ cup all-purpose flour

½ cup vegan butter cracker crumbs

A pinch of yellow cornmeal

4 tsps. very finely minced basil (Thai basil is OK)

1½ tsps. Old Bay or DFC Fish Fry Spice Mix (page 189)

SAUTÉ THE TEMPEH AND VEGGIES

1. Heat a 10-inch sauté pan on low for 4 minutes, add 1 tablespoon of the canola oil and heat for 1 minute. Add the shallots, bell pepper, and 2 cups of scallions to the pan and sauté for 2 minutes. Add the crumbled tempeh, garlic, Five Spice powder, Old Bay or DFC Fish Fry Spice Mix, sugar, and white pepper and stir until fragrant, about 3 minutes. Remove the pan from the heat, and transfer the mixture to a large bowl.

2. To the bowl, add the mayo, lemon juice, mustard, aminos, seaweed (if using), and crackers. Mix thoroughly. If the consistency is too wet, add more crackers..

Legendary rap unit Yo Majesty! is introduced to the wonders of tofu by DFC.

MAKE THE COATING

In a large bowl or shallow dish, combine all coating ingredients.

FRY THE PATTIES

1. Form the tofu mixture into 3-inch diameter patties, about the size of your palm. Coat each patty in the flour mixture and transfer to a plate. Let stand for 5 minutes before pan-frying.

2. In a 12-inch nonstick skillet set on medium, heat the remaining 2 tablespoons of oil until shimmering. Working in batches, gently place 6 patties into the skillet. Do not overcrowd the pan. Pan-fry until golden brown on both sides, about 4 minutes per side.

3. Transfer the patties to a warm plate and tent with foil to keep warm. If needed, wipe the skillet with paper towel and add 1 tablespoon of oil between batches. Serve immediately with a vegan version of Boujee Ranch Sauce (page 200). To make the vegan version, substitute vegan sour cream for the buttermilk and vegan mayo for the regular mayo, and add 2 tablespoons of nutritional yeast.

WE BAKE UP!

CHAPTER 4

SWEETS & QUICKBREADS

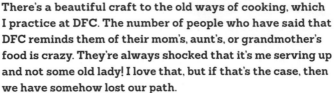

There's a beautiful craft to the old ways of cooking, which I practice at DFC. The number of people who have said that DFC reminds them of their mom's, aunt's, or grandmother's food is crazy. They're always shocked that it's me serving up and not some old lady! I love that, but if that's the case, then we have somehow lost our path.

Anyone who cherishes their time-tested family recipes has memories of being a kid and learning in their grandmother's kitchen, watching every move she made. My first food experiences are vividly linked to the blessed, sweet smell of oven-fresh coconut-honey biscuits. I remember pitting cherries for Grandma Jean's cherry pie and helping her with her amazing custards and puddings. Her blanched-peach cobbler was legendary, and you know I had to flip that recipe by adding lingonberries, which I first picked up in Sweden. I now substitute them for cranberries whenever I can; I'm addicted to their sour, yet lighter and more delicate, flavor.

That whole experience was special for me, way back when. Damn, I loved Grans' desserts. They inspired what I have for you here. Enjoy!

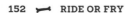

ORANGE COCONILLA PIE

I used to churn butter for the buttermilk used in this pie, one of my all-time favorites growing up. Churning is therapeutic, and I recommend it as a straight-up way to get back to basics. (You can always go to the store if you're out of time, though!) This dessert was only made for holidays, church functions, or other specific occasions, which made it feel extra special to me. The custard and cake-like layers in this pie combined with the orangey goodness remind me of cheesecake. Add a smothering of chocolate ganache and YUM! You've got an ultimate dessert on your hands.

SERVES **8 to 10**   PREP AND COOKING TIME **1 hour, 10 minutes plus refrigeration for 1 to 6 hours**

CRUST
- 6 tbsps. unsalted butter, chilled
- ½ cup yellow cornmeal
- 2 cups all-purpose flour
- A pinch of salt
- Grated zest of one orange
- 1 rounded tbsp. white sugar
- 4 tbsps. vegetable shortening, room temperature
- 4 tbsps. fresh orange juice, plus more as needed, chilled

FILLING
- 2 cups white sugar
- A pinch of salt
- Seeds from 2 vanilla beans
- ½ cup unsalted butter, at room temperature
- 4 to 5 rounded tbsps. all-purpose flour
- 3 large eggs, separated
- 1¼ cups buttermilk
- 1 tsp. cream of tartar (or lemon juice)

GANACHE
- 8 oz. bittersweet or dark chocolate, finely chopped
- ¾ cups heavy whipping cream
- Grated zest of one orange
- 2 tbsps. unsalted butter
- 1 tbsp. rum (light or dark)

PREPARE THE CRUST

1. To prepare the pie crust, freeze a large bowl, the butter, cornmeal, and flour for 30 minutes. If you don't have a marble or stainless steel surface on which to roll your dough, refrigerate a cutting board.

2. In the large, cold bowl combine the chilled flour, chilled cornmeal, salt, orange zest, and sugar.

3. Massage the vegetable shortening into the flour mixture until well combined.

ROLLING TIP

Don't just roll the dough back and forth. Try rolling north, pick up the pin, roll northeast; pick up dough and move counter-clockwise. Repeat. You want the crust as evenly rolled as possible. Continue to flour the surface underneath the dough to prevent sticking.

TRY THIS

An alternative method to transferring the crust to the pan is to gently fold the rolled-out dough in quarters, place the point in the center of the pie dish, and carefully unfold the dough.

4. Using a cheese grater, grate the chilled butter into the flour-shortening mixture, and toss to combine. It should look like a coarse cornmeal.

5. Sprinkle 1 tablespoon of the orange juice into flour-shortening mixture and toss it with a fork—do not touch the mixture with your hands. Repeat with remaining orange juice. Add more OJ as necessary, until mixture holds together when squeezed (see Alton's Trick).

6. Place dough in a large Ziploc bag, and squeeze it until a ball forms. Press dough into a disc and refrigerate for 30 minutes.

7. Divide refrigerated dough in half. You will only be using one half, so wrap up the other half and freeze it for another use. Flour your work surface, grab your rolling pin, and roll dough into a circle about 11 inches in diameter and ⅛ inch thick (see Rolling Tip).

8. To transfer to the pie dish, carefully wrap dough around rolling pin and center it above an ungreased, 9-inch pie dish. Carefully unroll dough onto the pie dish, and gently press it into the dish (see Note). Trim the excess dough. Go ahead, crimp it. Set aside.

MAKE THE FILLING

1. Preheat oven to 350°F.

2. Using a hand mixer or stand mixer fitted with the paddle attachment, cream the sugar, salt, vanilla seeds, and butter on medium speed, about 3 minutes. Stop mixer and scrape down the sides of the bowl. Add the flour and egg yolks, mix on medium for 1 minute. Add the buttermilk, mix until just combined.

3. In a chilled metal bowl, whip the egg whites with the cream of tartar or lemon juice until soft peaks form. Fold egg whites into buttermilk mixture and pour the batter into the pie shell.

BAKE THE PIE

1. Bake pie for 45 to 50 minutes, or until a toothpick inserted in the center comes out clean. The top should be slightly crusty and brown.

2. Cool pie completely on a wire rack, and refrigerate it for 3 hours or up to overnight.

MAKE THE GANACHE

1. To make the ganache, place the chocolate in a medium stainless steel bowl.

2. In a 4-quart sauce pan set on medium-high, heat the cream, orange zest, and butter. Bring mixture to a slow boil. Immediately pour the boiling cream over the chocolate and allow to stand for 5 minutes, then whisk until smooth. Stir in the rum, if using.

3. Spread the ganache over the chilled pie and let set, about 1 hour. I serve the CocoNilla with fresh whipped cream flavored with vanilla.

T~~T~~ THEOPHILUS ~~T~~'S LONDON 👓
CHOCOLATE PUMPKIN PIE!

This pie was inspired by Theophilus London, one of my favorite recording artists and an all-around cool dude. He's one of those New Yorkers who makes you proud to live there. When Theophilus was a guest on my show, we talked a lot about his Trinidadian/Caribbean heritage, including the food he ate growing up. Then we cooked up this pie, which has basic ingredients that can be found in Caribbean cooking, and I named it in honor of him. All I gots to say is, combine chocolate, coconut, and pumpkin with some warm spices and then put it all in your mouth. Yum! You can make a non-vegan version of this, too, but you really don't need to.

SERVES **6 to 8**   PREP AND COOKING TIME **1 ½ hours**

CRUST

- 1 12-oz. box vegan ginger snaps, or your favorite cookie
- ¼ cup white sugar
  A pinch of sea salt
- ¼ tsp. ground ginger
- 6 tbsps. Earth Balance Natural Buttery Spread, melted **or**
- 1 9-inch vegan premade cookie pie crust

FILLING

- 1 15-oz. can of puréed pumpkin
- 1 cup thick coconut milk
- 1 tsp. coconut butter
- ¼ cup (packed) light brown sugar
- 1 cup molasses
- ½ tsp. sea salt
- 1 tbsp. cinnamon
  A pinch of ground ginger
  A pinch of ground cloves
  A pinch of freshly grated nutmeg
  A pinch of allspice
- 1 tbsp. Earth Balance Natural Buttery Spread
- 1½ tsps. potato starch or cornstarch

TOPPING

- 1 to 1½ cups sweetened coconut flakes
- ¾ cup thick coconut milk
  8-oz. unsweetened dark chocolate, chopped
  Vegan whipped topping, such as Soyatoo's Rice Whip

MAKE THE CRUST

1. Preheat oven to 350°F.
2. If making your own crust, place half of the gingersnaps in a food processor and reduce to a fine crumb. Add the sugar, salt, and ginger. Pulse to combine. Add the Earth Balance to the crumbs and process until crumbly. Press the crumbs evenly into a 9-inch pie plate. Bake for 8 minutes. Set on a wire rack to cool. Leave the oven on.

MAKE THE FILLING AND BAKE UP

1. In a blender, add the pumpkin, coconut milk, coconut butter, brown sugar, molasses, salt, cinnamon, ginger, cloves, nutmeg, allspice, Earth Balance, and starch and process until smooth.

Theophilus London with his namesake pie: a flavor shout-out to his Trinidadian roots.

2. Pour pumpkin mixture into the cooled pie crust, place in on a rimmed baking sheet, and bake for about 60 minutes. The pie will still be jiggly when you take it out of the oven, but it will firm up as it cools. Cool completely on a wire rack for 1 hour before applying the topping ingredients

MAKE THE TOPPING
1. Preheat oven to 350°F.
2. Spread the coconut in a single layer on a baking sheet. Toast until brown, about 7 minutes. Transfer the toasted coconut to a small bowl.
3. In a small sauce pan set on medium-high, heat the coconut milk until just boiling. Remove the pan from the heat and add the chocolate and let stand for 5 minutes. Using a spatula, mix until smooth.
4. Spread the chocolate mixture over the cooled pie, then sprinkle with the toasted coconut. Insert about 8 to 10 toothpicks around the edge of the pie (this will create supports to protect topping from sticking to tented plastic wrap), cover with plastic wrap, and refrigerate for several hours or overnight before serving.

SERVE
Serve chilled, topped with vegan whipped topping and a pinch of cracked black pepper.

→PEACH-N-LINGONBERRY

 COBBLER

This is an old-timey recipe that I updated by adding toasted pecans to the crust and substituting lingonberries for cranberries. The crust has an awesome nutty flavor and the light, slightly sour flavor of the lingonberries mixes perfectly with the peaches. (I don't hate on cranberries so no worries if you can't find lingonberries.) Serve warm with sour or whipped cream, ice cream, or cottage cheese.

SERVES **10 to 12**   PREP AND COOKING TIME **1 hour**

CRUST

Follow Orange CocoNilla crust recipe (page 153, omit the orange zest)

1 cup pecans, toasted, coarsely crushed, and coated in flour

FILLING

10 to 12 medium peaches, pitted, peeled, and sliced (see Note)

1 ½ cups dried lingonberries or dried cranberries
   Juice of ½ a lemon

¾ cup orange juice, preferably freshly squeezed

½ cup plus 1 tbsp. unsalted butter

½ cup pure maple syrup

1 ½ cups plus 1 tbsp. white sugar

½ tsp. freshly grated nutmeg

1 tbsp. ground cinnamon

2 tbsps. cornstarch or potato starch

MAKE THE CRUST

1. Preheat oven to 350°F. Make pie crust according to the directions on page 153, substituting the pecans for the orange zest.
2. On a lightly floured surface roll out half of dough into a 10 x 14-inch rectangle, about ⅛ inch thick.
3. Press dough into a 9 x 13-inch baking dish. It should cover bottom and halfway up the sides. Prick dough all over with a fork.
4. Bake crust until golden brown, about 20 minutes. Carefully set crust on a wire rack to cool.

Fill a large stock pot halfway with water and bring to boil. Submerge the peaches in the boiling water for 1 minute. Drain. Run peaches under cold water. The skin will easily peel off.

MAKE THE FILLING

1. In a 9-inch sauce pan set on medium-low, combine the peaches, lingonberries, lemon juice, and orange juice. Add ½ cup butter and the maple syrup and cook until butter is melted, about 8 minutes.

2. In a small mixing bowl, combine 1½ cups sugar, nutmeg, cinnamon, and starch. Add to peach mixture, stirring to combine. Remove from heat, and pour filling into the cooled crust.

MAKE THE LATTICE

1. Preheat oven to 450°F.

2. Roll remaining dough into a 10 x 14-inch rectangle, about ⅛ inch thick.

3. Using a knife or pastry wheel, cut dough into 10 1-inch-wide strips. Lay four evenly spaced strips lengthwise on top of the cobbler. Now lay six evenly spaced strips crosswise on top of the cobbler, forming the lattice. Use a sharp knife or kitchen shears to trim any overhanging dough.

4. Just before baking, melt remaining 1 tablespoon butter. With a pastry brush, dab lattice with melted butter. Sprinkle remaining 1 tablespoon sugar over butter-coated lattice.

BAKE UP

Bake cobbler for 10 minutes, then reduce heat to 350°F and continue baking until crust is golden brown, about 25 minutes more. Serve warm.

YAM PARTY PIE

This dessert is a play on the candied yam casserole I ate growing up. I took the original version and developed it as a pie while working on a series of New York City parties centered around new pie concepts. This insane concoction tastes just like a candy bar—take a bite and your sweet tooth will beg you for more. It became an instant hit with the crowds in NYC, and why wouldn't it? Yams like to party too.

SERVES **8 to 10**   PREP AND COOKING TIME **1 hour 40 minutes**

1 crust from Theophilus London Chocolate Pumpkin Pie (page 156), made with cookies of your choice, **or**
1 9-inch store-bought cookie crust
½ cup (1 stick) unsalted butter
4 medium sweet potatoes, peeled and quartered (skins left on)
1 cup (packed) light brown sugar
1 cup water

1 thumb-size piece of fresh ginger, peeled and minced
2 cinnamon sticks
A pinch of nutmeg
A pinch of salt
1 cup salted mixed nuts
½ cup pure maple syrup or agave nectar
1 cup salted pretzels, crushed
½ cup semisweet chocolate chips

5 dried apricots, minced
2 1½-oz. toffee candy bars (Heath bar, for instance), crushed
1 cup salted popcorn, coarsely chopped
2 large eggs, separated
1 cup heavy cream or whole milk
3 tbsps. malted milk powder
2 cups mini marshmallows
½ cup confectioners' sugar, for garnish

1. Preheat oven to 350°F.
2. In a 10-inch cast-iron skillet or nonstick frying pan set on medium, melt the butter. Add the sweet potatoes, brown sugar, water, ginger, cinnamon sticks, nutmeg, salt, and maple syrup, and cook on low heat for one hour, stirring frequently, until sweet potatoes are candied and the mixture is bubbling. Remove and discard cinnamon sticks.
3. Transfer mixture to a blender and purée until smooth. Scrape purée into a large bowl and let cool to room temperature.
4. While purée cools, prep the nuts. Toss nuts in maple syrup or agave and spread on a large, rimmed baking sheet. Toast them until fragrant, about 15 minutes. Remove nuts from oven and let cool on a small plate. Coarsely chop the cooled nuts. Leave the oven on.
5. In a medium bowl, combine the nuts, pretzels, chocolate chips, apricots, toffee bars, and popcorn. Set aside.
6. In a medium bowl, beat the eggs whites until soft peaks form.

7. In a large bowl whisk together the cream or milk, egg yolks, and malted milk powder. Stir in the cooled sweet potato purée, then fold in the egg whites.

8. Very gently fold the nut mixture into the purée mixture.

9. Pour filling into the pie shell, stopping just before the filling meets the edge, taking care not to overfill the shell.

10. Place pie on a baking sheet and bake for 25 minutes. Carefully remove pie from oven.

11. Sprinkle the marshmallows over top of the pie, and return it to oven to bake for another 20 to 30 minutes, until marshmallows are melted and browned.

12. Cool pie completely on a wire rack. Chill it if you are not serving the pie until the next day. Dust the pie with the confectioners' sugar just before serving.

GINGER-PINEAPPLE UPSIDE-DOWN CAKE

I've loved this dessert my whole life. The warmth of the cake combined with molasses and the ooey-gooey caramelized fruit is so damn good. The ginger flavor makes me think of the awesome ginger cake tradition they have in the UK during the holidays—they're serious about that thing. So here's a special invitation to all my UK friends, fam, and fans: indulge in this one too.

SERVES **8 to 10**   PREP AND COOKING TIME **1 ½ hours**

UPSIDE DOWN TOPPING
- 5 tbsps. unsalted butter
- 1 tsp. minced fresh ginger
- 1 8-oz. can pineapple rings, drained with juice reserved (about ¼ cup)
- ½ cup brown sugar
- 8 to 10 fresh or frozen cherries, pitted

BATTER
- 1 tsp. cinnamon
- 2 tsps. minced candied pineapple
- 1 tsp. ground ginger
- ½ tsp. ground cloves
- ⅓ tsp. allspice
- ½ tsp. sea salt
- 2 cups all-purpose flour

- ½ cup lard or (1 stick) unsalted butter
- 1 cup molasses
- ½ cup light brown sugar, packed
- 1 tsp. minced candied ginger
- 2 large eggs
- 1 cup boiling water
- 1 tsp. baking soda

Preheat oven to 350°F.

MAKE UPSIDE-DOWN TOPPING
In a 10-inch ovenproof frying pan or cast-iron skillet set on medium, melt the butter. Stir in the minced ginger and remove from the heat. Sprinkle in the pineapple juice and brown sugar. Place the pineapple rings evenly in the pan and place a cherry in the center of each ring. Any remaining rings can be cut in half and propped along the sides of the pan like arches. Set the pan aside.

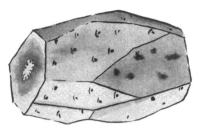

MAKE THE BATTER

1. In a small bowl combine the cinnamon, candied pineapple, ginger, cloves, allspice, salt, and flour.
2. In large bowl cream the lard or butter, molasses, brown sugar, and minced candied ginger with a hand mixer or whisk until light and fluffy, about 3 minutes.
3. Add the eggs, mixing to combine thoroughly.
4. Slowly add dry ingredients to the creamed mixture. Mix well.
5. In a small bowl, combine the boiling water and the baking soda.
6. Quickly whisk the baking soda mixture into the batter.

BAKE UP

Pour the batter into a greased and floured 9-inch cake pan (being careful not to overfill) and bake until a toothpick inserted in the center of the cake comes out clean, about 28 to 33 minutes. Let the cake cool for 10 minutes. Place a serving platter larger than the pan on top of the cake. Using a butter knife, gently free the cake from the edges of the pan and then carefully invert the pan and platter together to release the cake onto the platter. Serve warm with whipped cream or ice cream.

KATE'S BOOTLEG (TOFU) CAKE

I once worked at Kate's Joint vegetarian dinner on the Lower East Side of NYC, a vegetarian greasy spoon with a smoking section and late-night, debauched behavior. (Come on, that's sick!) There was so much awesome food. I went downright bananas for Kate's tofu cheesecake and vegan whipped "cream." Kate's never given up those recipes (I don't blame her), so this is the DFC take. I hope she approves. If you're in New York, definitely hit up the diner—their killer club sandwich and nachos are the best vegan versions I've ever had.

SERVES **8**   PREP AND COOKING TIME **2¾ hours, plus 2 hours to overnight for chilling**

1 crust from Theophilus London Chocolate Pumpkin Pie (page 156), made with vegan graham crackers, **or** premade vegan cookie pie crust

FILLING
1 12-oz. package of silken tofu
¼ cup tofu cream cheese
⅓ to 1 cup thick coconut milk
  Seeds from 1 vanilla bean
3 tbsps. pure maple syrup

2 tbsps. almond butter
3 cups vegan marshmallows
½ cup confectioners' sugar
1 tsp. sea salt
2 tbsps. fresh lemon juice
1 tsp. egg replacer powder (prepared according to instructions on the box)
5 tbsps. peanut oil or melted Earth Balance

TOPPING
¾ cup coconut milk
8 oz. vegan white chocolate, chopped
1 tbsp. water
2 cups fresh raspberries

SPECIAL EQUIPMENT
  9-inch tart pan with removable bottom

Preheat oven to 325°F.

MAKE THE FILLING

1. Place a paper towel in a small bowl, and put the tofu on top. Then wrap the top of the tofu in another paper towel. Let it drain for 15 minutes. Repeat this process, if you want. Draining the tofu makes its texture creamier when puréed.
2. In a blender, add the tofu, tofu cream cheese, coconut milk, vanilla seeds, maple syrup, almond butter, marshmallows, confectioners' sugar, salt, lemon juice, and prepared egg replacer. Process until thick and creamy. With the blender on a low speed, slowly incorporate the oil or melted Earth Balance.
3. Pour filling into the prepared crust, leaving just a little crust exposed. Do not overfill.

BAKE UP

Bake the cheesecake on the middle rack until the top of is shiny but the center is still slightly wobbly when pan is gently shaken, about 1 hour. Turn off oven, and leave the cheesecake in the oven 1 hour more. Transfer to a wire rack and let it cool to room temperature, about 45 minutes.

MAKE THE TOPPING

1. While the cheesecake is cooling, make the topping. In a small sauce pan set on medium-high, bring the coconut milk to a boil. Place the chocolate in a small bowl. Pour the boiling coconut milk over the chocolate and let stand for 5 minutes. Use a spatula to whisk until smooth.

2. Spread the chocolate sauce evenly over the cheesecake, and top with the fresh raspberries. Refrigerate for 2 to 6 hours, or up to overnight. Serve cold (do not let it come to room temperature) with whipped tofu topping.

OUDWEE'S COCONUT-BANANA GRITS

These grits are inspired by the Filipino sticky banana rice that my best friend Jon Jon's grandmother made when we were kids—I loved the exotic taste of it. I think it works best as a dessert, even though it was traditionally served up with dinner. (You can serve it with dinner too if you'd like—just make the recipe less sweet by decreasing the amount of sugar or agave nectar, or leave it out entirely.) Who is Oudwee? She's my cousin who loves grits. This is a DFC favorite; I hope you like it too.

SERVES **4 to 6**   PREP AND COOKING TIME **45 minutes**

½ cup sweetened coconut flakes
1 ½ cups coconut milk
2 bananas, 1 whole and 1 sliced into ¼-inch-thick pieces
1 20-oz. can of crushed pineapple, drained

1 ½ cups water
  A pinch of sea salt
4 tbsps. unsalted butter

1 cup stone ground grits (not quick cook; polenta or yellow grits are OK substitutes)
1 cup white sugar or agave nectar

1. Preheat oven to 375°F.
2. Arrange the coconut flakes in a single layer on a rimmed baking sheet. Toast coconut until golden brown, about 10 minutes. Transfer to a small bowl and set aside.
3. In a blender, purée the coconut milk, the whole banana, pineapple, water, and salt.
4. Transfer mixture to a 6-quart pot and bring to boil.
5. Meanwhile, in small pan on medium, sauté 2 tablespoons butter and the sliced banana for 3 minutes. Remove from heat.
6. Slowly add the grits to coconut-milk mixture, whisking constantly to break up lumps. Add sugar or agave, reduce heat to low, and simmer grits for 10 to 15 minutes (if using polenta, make it a little longer), stirring frequently.
7. Add sautéed bananas, stirring gently to combine. Serve up the grits immediately, garnished with toasted coconut.

SOCK-IT-TO-ME! AMBROSIA SALAD

Ambrosia means food of the gods, though truth be told, the gods did not have my back when I was a kid. Why? Well, for one thing, the other young'uns and I weren't served this dish, made from one of the crack recipes in my family. Instead, the adults and teenagers would get their fill first, leaving a horde of kids to attack the dessert bowl like desperate hyenas fighting over remnants of sauce and scraps of fruit. When I got older I realized that the majority of ambrosia recipes are made with some gross, processed Kool Whip steez. I'm proud we always honored the gods by using fresh ingredients. Eco fresh, yo!

SERVES 6   PREP AND COOKING TIME **1 hour and 20 minutes**

- 1 13.5-oz. can of coconut milk
- ½ cup white sugar
- 1 11-oz. can of mandarin oranges in light syrup, drained
- 2 cups fresh pineapple chunks, minced
- 1 large banana, sliced into ½-inch-thick slices
- ½ cup seedless grapes, halved

- ½ cup blackberries
- 1 cup whole strawberries, hulled, and chopped into ½-inch pieces
- ½ small cantaloupe, balled with a melon baller (about 2 cups)
- 2 doughnut peaches, pitted and sliced into ½-inch pieces
- 1 cup sweetened shredded coconut, toasted

- 1 cup almonds or pecans, toasted
- 2 cups mini marshmallows, toasted
- ¾ cup sour cream
- 2 tbsps. pure maple syrup
- 1 cup dried sour cherries

SPECIAL EQUIPMENT
  Melon baller
  Kitchen torch

1. In a 4-quart sauce pan set on medium-low, gently heat the coconut milk. Add the sugar and stir until dissolved. Simmer until volume is reduced by half, about 1 hour. Remove from heat, transfer to a bowl, and let the mixture cool completely. Refrigerate reduced coconut milk until you are ready to serve the salad.
2. While coconut milk is thickening, preheat oven to 375°F and combine all of your prepped fresh fruit in a large bowl. Cover and refrigerate.

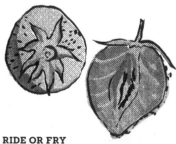

3. On separate rimmed baking sheets, spread the coconut and nuts in single layers. Toast for 10 minutes. Watch it! This stuff goes from fragrant to burnt pretty quickly. Set aside the toasted coconut and nuts.

4. Arrange the marshmallows on a heat-resistant plate. Using a kitchen torch, toast one side of the marshmallows and then the other. Set aside.

5. Immediately before serving, add the sour cream (or your dairy of choice) and the maple syrup to the reduced coconut milk, stirring to combine.

6. Add the nuts, dried cherries, and toasted marshmallows to the fruit bowl, stirring to combine. Pour the coconut milk mixture over the fruit and gently fold in the dressing. I top each serving with fresh whipped cream.

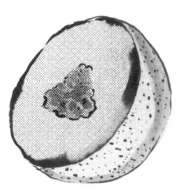

STRAWBERRY-N-CHOCOLATE CUPCAKES

OH YES!

When I worked at Herbivore in San Francisco, a hugely popular vegan restaurant in The Bay, I was inspired by their super dense, moist chocolate cupcakes. Those things were the ultimate! Herbivore garnished theirs with a sliced strawberry; I kept the slice and did my own fruit power move by adding strawberry preserves (homemade is best, of course, if you can swing it) to the mix, as well as a heap of dried strawberries.

MAKES **12 cupcakes**   PREP AND COOKING TIME **1½ hour**

BATTER
1   cup soy milk
1   tsp. apple cider vinegar, preferably Bragg's
1   cup white sugar
½   cup plus 2 tbsps. Earth Balance Natural Buttery Spread, at room temperature
1   tsp. vanilla extract
½   tsp. almond extract
1½ cups all-purpose flour
⅓   cup cocoa powder, preferably Dutch-process
¾   tsp. baking soda
½   tsp. baking powder
¼   tsp. sea salt

FILLING
2   cups strawberry preserves, puréed

TOPPING
8-oz. unsweetened dark chocolate, chopped
4   dried strawberries, minced
¾   cup thick coconut milk
2   tbsps. Earth Balance Natural Buttery Spread
6   large strawberries, halved

SPECIAL EQUPIMENT
12-cup muffin tin cupcake liners
Squirt bottle
Pastry bag fitted with large tip

MAKE THE BATTER
1. Preheat oven to 350°F. Line a 12-cup muffin pan with paper or foil liners.
2. In a large bowl, whisk the soy milk and vinegar. Set aside for a few minutes to curdle.
3. In medium bowl, cream the sugar and ½ cup Earth Balance and add the vanilla and almond extracts, mixing until just incorporated. Add the butter mixture to the soy milk mixture and beat until foamy.
4. In a medium bowl, sift together the flour, cocoa powder, baking soda, baking powder, and salt.
5. Add half of the flour mixture to the butter mixture, and beat with a whisk (or electric hand mixer on low) until incorporated. Beat in the remaining flour mixture. The batter should be free of large lumps (a few tiny lumps are cool).

BAKE UP

Fill the cupcake liner three-quarters full with batter. Bake until a toothpick inserted into the center comes out clean, about 18 to 20 minutes. Transfer the pan to a cooling rack and let the cupcakes cool for 10 minutes. Pop the cupcakes out of the pan to cool completely.

MAKE THE TOPPING

1. Place the chopped chocolate and minced strawberries in medium bowl.

2. In a small sauce pan, heat the coconut milk until just about boiling, then pour it over the chocolate and strawberries. With a spatula, stir the mixture until smooth. Let cool to room temperature; it will thicken as it cools. The texture should thick, but spreadable, like very soft fudge.

3. Load the topping into a pastry bag fitted with the large tip or a Ziploc bag with one corner snipped off. Refrigerate the pastry bag until needed.

FILL 'ER UP AND FROST

1. Fill a squirt bottle with the puréed preserves. Insert the tip of the squirt bottle as far as it will go into the center of each cooled cupcake, and squirt a little (or a lot if you like) preserves into each cupcake.

2. Squeezing from the bottom of the pastry or Ziploc bag, frost each filled cupcake with the chocolate topping in a swirl starting from the outside and working inward. Garnish each cupcake with a strawberry slice. Refrigerate the dressed up cupcakes for an hour or two before serving.

COCONUT-HONEY BISCUITS

These biscuits are a legendary DFC staple. They're so good that if I don't have them at my parties, there's anarchy. There's nothing new about how I make these biscuits, like a lot of baking, it is a matter of using tried-and-true recipe and technique. That said, we still flip this 'ish with dried coconut and glaze it with raw, dripping honey right out of the hot oven. They're beyond incredible.

MAKES **10 to 12 biscuits**   PREP AND COOKING TIME **40 minutes**

2½ cups all-purpose flour, plus more for the board
3 tsps. baking powder
1 tsp. sea salt
1 cup coconut flakes, chilled
3 tbsps. nonhydrogenated vegetable shortening, at room temperature

6 tbsps. (¾ of a stick) unsalted butter, chilled in freezer for 20 minutes
1 cup buttermilk

TOPPING
½ cup honey
2 tbsps. unsalted butter

SPECIAL EQUIPMENT
2-inch biscuit or cookie cutter

TRY GLOVES

I find that wearing food handlers' gloves prevents the dough from sticking to my fingers, plus the dough stays cooler.

MAKE THE DOUGH

1. Preheat oven to 425°F.
2. In a medium bowl, sift the flour, baking powder, and salt together. Add the coconut flakes, tossing with a fork to combine.
3. Add the shortening to the flour mixture and using your hands, quickly combine.
4. With a box grater, grate the butter into the flour-shortening mixture and toss with a fork.
5. Form a well in the center of the flour and add the buttermilk into the well, and toss with a fork until a thick dough forms.
6. Turn dough out onto a floured surface (see Note). Gently knead the dough 2 or 3 times and roll or pat it into a ½-inch-thick rectangle or round. If the dough is too sticky, sprinkle a little flour on top. If it's too dry, add a little more buttermilk.

CHILL WITH THE BISCUITS

Biscuits can be tricky. You must keep all the ingredients (except the shortening) cold and move with the speed of light when mixing. I even chill the flour in the freezer. A marble countertop is the perfect surface for kneading and cutting biscuits, but if that's not happening, chill your cutting board. When the cold ingredients hit the heat of the oven, the fluffy, flaky, tender goodness happens.

7. With a floured 2-inch biscuit cutter or large drinking glass, cut out your biscuits. Gently scrunch the scraps into a mound and cut more biscuits. These are the "scrap" biscuits. They will not be as tender as the first biscuits you cut, but they are still the bomb.

BAKE AND COAT

1. Place the unbaked biscuits ½ inch apart on an ungreased baking sheet. Bake until golden brown, 12 to 20 minutes.
2. While the biscuits are baking, heat the remaining butter and the honey in small sauce pan.
3. When biscuits are done, immediately coat them with the honey-butter using a pastry brush.

GARLIC-RHUBARB HUSH PUPPIES

Everybody loves hush puppies, and I've had so many variations that I've lost count. This version has an awesome combination of spicy and savory notes; the crisp, fresh jalapeño and the soft, stewed rhubarb create an ideal balance. Hush puppies are a great complement to a wide range of stuff, including catfish and gumbo; they're also delicious served with soups and stews.

MAKES **about 15 hush puppies**

PREP AND COOKING TIME **40 minutes**

- 1 tbsp. unsalted butter or olive oil
- 2 rhubarb stalks, minced
- 1 small red onion, chopped
- 3 garlic gloves, minced
- 2 green onions, minced
- 1 jalapeño or mild chili, ribs and seeds removed, minced
- 2 tbsps. white sugar
  Water
- 1 cup yellow cornmeal
- 3 tbsps. all-purpose flour
- 3 tsps. baking powder
- ¼ tsp. baking soda

- 1 tsp. veggie bouillon
- ½ tsp. sea salt
- 1 tsp. allspice
- 1 tbsp. chili powder
- 1 large egg, beaten

- ¾ cup buttermilk
- 4 to 5 cups canola or peanut oil
  Honey

SPECIAL EQUIPMENT
Candy thermometer

MAKE THE DOUGH

1. In a 10-inch skillet set on medium, add the butter or oil, rhubarb, onion, red garlic, green onion, and jalapeño and sauté until translucent, about 5 minutes. Add the sugar and just enough water to cover the bottom of the skillet. Raise the heat to high and stir until water has evaporated, 5 minutes more. Remove from heat and set aside.
2. In a large bowl, whisk together the cornmeal, flour, baking powder, baking soda, bouillon, salt, allspice, and chili powder.
3. In a medium bowl, combine the beaten egg, buttermilk, and sautéed rhubarb mixture.
4. Add the wet ingredients to the cornmeal mixture, stirring to combine. The mixture should hold together but not be doughy. Let it rest for 5 minutes.

FRY THE PUPPIES

1. Prepare a deep fryer according the directions or fill a deep, heavy-bottomed pot with 3 inches of the oil and heat to 350°F. Check the oil temperature with a candy thermometer.
2. Working in batches, drop the batter by the tablespoon into the hot oil. Fry, turning halfway through, until the hush puppies are golden brown, about 3 to 5 minutes. With a slotted spoon, carefully remove the puppies from the oil and place them on newspaper or paper towels to drain.
3. Drizzle with honey and serve warm. Serve with Jean's Slow-School Chili (pages 55), Jean's Cook-Up Gumbo (page 58), or Yam-Banana Catfish (page 67).

PINEAPPLE DINNER ROLLS

Yeasty rolls are my favorite dinner bread, hands down. There's no denying the greatness of a sweet, buttery roll with a meal. Thank God these are kind of dramatic to make, because if I came up with a shortcut, I would be a fat bastard. For real. When my granny made these, we called them Hawaiian onion rolls, and they were the source of scuffles in my family. You might want to double, or even triple, this recipe because they're addictive—turn your back, and they're gone.

MAKES **24 rolls**   PREP AND COOKING TIME **3 hours**

3 tbsps. dehydrated pineapple, minced
2 tbsp. dried shallots
1 tbsps. poppy seeds
4 cups all-purpose flour
1¼ cups buttermilk, warm
¼ cup warm water

½ cup white sugar
1 tsp. sea salt
1 package active dry yeast
½ cup (1 stick) plus 3 tbsps. unsalted butter, at room temperature

1 tbsp. nonhydrogenated vegetable shortening, at room temperature
1 large egg, beaten

TOPPING
3 tbsps. unsalted butter
½ to 1 tbsp. honey or agave nectar

WARM UP

It's best to make these rolls on warm days because the yeast won't activate if it's too cool. If you are making these rolls during the winter, your kitchen should be nice and toasty. The oven can help warm the room.

MAKE THE DOUGH

1. In a medium bowl, combine the pineapple, shallots, poppy seeds, and flour.
2. In small bowl, combine the buttermilk, water, sugar, salt, yeast, ½ cup of the butter, and the shortening. Stir well. Set aside for 5 minutes. Stir in the beaten egg.
3. In the bowl of a stand mixer fitted with the dough hook, combine the yeast mixture and ½ cup of the flour mixture. Mix on medium speed until the flour is incorporated, about 1 minute. Add the remaining flour ½ cup at a time, continuing to mix on medium speed. The dough should be smooth and elastic. The texture should feel like a cross between Play-Doh and marshmallows (see Note).
4. Transfer the dough to a large, greased glass bowl, and cover it with plastic wrap. Let the dough rise until doubled, about 1½ hours.

WHEN MIXING BY HAND

If you are mixing the dough by hand: In large mixing bowl, combine the buttermilk, water, sugar, salt, yeast, 1/2 cup butter, and 1 tbsp. shortening. Stir mixture with a spoon to blend well. Set aside for 5 minutes. Stir in the beaten egg. Add the flour mixture, 1/2 cup at a time. When the dough gets too stiff to mix with a spoon, turn it out onto a floured surface and knead by hand for 5 to 6 minutes, gradually adding remaining flour, until smooth and elastic.

MAKE THE ROLLS

1. In a small pan, melt the 3 tablespoons butter.
2. Divide the risen dough in half and place one half on a floured surface. Roll the dough into a 12-inch disc that is about 1/8 inch thick.
3. Cut the disc into 12 wedges, butter each wedge with pastry brush, and roll up each wedge from the wide end to the narrow end to form a crescent roll.
4. Place the rolls 1 inch apart on a greased baking sheet. Cover loosely with plastic wrap or a clean kitchen towel and let rise, about 45 minutes.

BAKE THE ROLLS

1. Preheat oven to 325°F degrees.
2. Brush the risen rolls with the remaining butter. Bake until lightly golden, 12 to 15 minutes.

TOP 'EM OFF

As the biscuits are baking, melt the butter and honey or agave. When the biscuits come out of the oven, give them a coating of honey-butter. Serve warm.

GINGER SPICE CORNBREAD

So many cornbread lovers scratch their heads at this one, perplexed by the warm spice—the cheery holiday feel—of the cinnamon, nutmeg, and ginger notes. It's cornbread, for sure, but different. Perfect with a little maple syrup on top, I suggest double dipping it in soup, gravy, or chili. Whatever you do, get it into your mouth ASAP. I always try to use a cast-iron skillet when making cornbread so I can get that ultimate crispy-burnt crust. (If you don't own a cast-iron skillet already, I highly recommend investing in one. It's hella versatile cookware and will last forever.)

SERVES 8   PREP AND COOKING TIME **1½ hour**

GINGER SPICE
½ red bell pepper, ribs and
   seeds removed, minced
½ small red onion, minced
½ cup cooked corn,
   preferably fresh
½ thumb-size piece of fresh
   ginger, peeled and minced
1 jalapeño, ribs and seeds
   removed, minced (optional)
1½ tsps. ground cumin

1½ tsps. cinnamon
   A pinch of ground cloves
1 tbsp. chili powder
   Water

CORNBREAD
1½ cups coarse
   yellow cornmeal
½ cup all-purpose flour
1½ tsps. baking powder
¼ cup white sugar

1 tsp. sea salt
2 large eggs
5 tbsps. unsalted butter or
   bacon drippings
1¼ cups buttermilk
1 tbsp. peanut or canola oil

TOPPING
1 tbsp. unsalted butter,
   at room temperature
2 tbsps. pure maple syrup

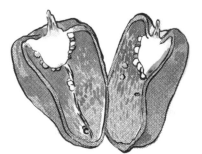

MAKE THE GINGER SPICE
In a 10-inch skillet set on medium heat, sauté the bell pepper, onion, corn, ginger, and jalapeño, until translucent, about 5 minutes. Add the cumin, cinnamon, cloves, and chili powder, stirring to combine. Add a little water to make a paste. Transfer the mixture to a small bowl to cool.

MIX AND BAKE

1. Preheat oven to 400°F.
2. In a large bowl combine the cornmeal, flour, baking powder, sugar, and salt.
3. In a medium bowl, combine the eggs, butter or bacon drippings, and buttermilk. Add this mixture to the cornmeal mixture, stirring until the batter is just blended. Lumps are OK.
4. Heat a 12-inch cast-iron skillet on high for 2 minutes. Add the oil and swirl it around the skillet to coat the bottom and sides. Heat for 1 minute more.
5. Pour the cornbread batter into the skillet and cook on high heat until bubbles start to form in the center, about 2 minutes. Remove the skillet from the heat and place on middle rack in preheated oven.
6. Bake until a knife inserted into the center comes out clean, about 40 to 50 minutes.

TOP AND SERVE

Remove the skillet from the oven and spread the butter over top. Drizzle with the maple syrup. Let the cornbread cool for a few minutes, cut into wedges, and serve.

COOL SIPS

SIPS

CHAPTER 5

ALOE-GINGER LEMONADE

This earthy, addictive thirst quencher raises the bar on strawberry lemonade by including aloe instead. Aloe is an incredible thing—stop sleeping on it! Use that stuff, pronto. It's good for you and has a light sweetness that reminds me of lychee juice (which is a good substitute for aloe in this recipe). The swagged-out version is laced with vodka or sake.

MAKES **about 1 gallon**   PREP TIME **45 minutes**

11½ cups water
1   thumb-size piece of fresh
    ginger peeled and grated
1½ cups sugar, raw or refined
2   7-oz. bottles of TGK
    aloe vera drink (see Note)

Juice of 12 to 15 lemons,
2   lemon rinds, pith removed
¼ cup apple cider vinegar,
    preferably Bragg's
    Vodka, preferably Ketel One,
    to taste (optional)

You can find TGK aloe vera juice all throughout the U.S. and EU. It's available online as well. There are other brands, but most contain high-fructose corn syrup.

1. In a small sauce pan set on high, combine 1½ cups water, the ginger, and sugar. Bring to a boil, and let the mixture bubble until sugar is dissolved, about 3 minutes. Remove from heat and let it cool 20 minutes.

2. In a 1-gallon vessel with a lid, combine the aloe drink, lemon juice, lemon rinds, apple cider vinegar, and the remaining water. Add the cooled ginger syrup, close the lid, and shake vigorously to combine. Refrigerate until cold, or serve immediately over ice. If you want to get your swerve on, fill a martini shaker with ice and 1 cup of lemonade. Add a shot (1½ ounces) of vodka, shake well, and serve in a martini glass.

PEACH COBBLER QUENCHER

One sweaty summer in Harlem I had a grip of fresh peaches from upstate New York that were begging to be used. It was way too hot for the peach cobbler bake-off that I was fiending for, and you know how I roll—I couldn't let that awesome fruit go to waste. The NYC heat wave had everyone mad thirsty, so I decided to make a drinkable peach cobbler with a splash of vodka. You can also swap in rum or whiskey if that's your tipple of choice.

MAKES **about 1 gallon**   PREP TIME **1 hour**

PEELING PEACHES

Fill a large stock pot halfway with water and bring to boil. Submerge the peaches in the boiling water for 1 minute. Drain. Run peaches under cold water. The skin will easily peel off.

SWEET!

Instead of sugar, you can use a natural sweetener, such as honey, maple syrup, or agave nectar.

2 cups frozen peaches or
   4 fresh peaches peeled,
   pitted, and sliced (see Note)
1½ cups fresh or frozen
   cranberries
2 cups sugar

2 cinnamon sticks
10 cups water
   64 oz. fresh-squeezed orange juice
   Rum, vodka, or whiskey, to taste
   (optional)

1. In a 6 quart stock pot set on high, combine the peaches, cranberries, sugar, and cinnamon sticks. Bring to a boil. Reduce the heat to low and simmer for 30 minutes. Remove from heat, remove the cinnamon sticks, and let the mixture cool for 20 minutes.
2. Pour one-third of the stewed peach mixture into a blender and add about one-third of the orange juice (do not overfill). Purée until smooth. Pour the purée into your pitcher or container. Repeat the process 2 more times with the remaining fruit and juice.
3. Adjust sweetness by adding more sugar or water.
4. Serve the cobbler drink over ice. For a cocktail, fill a martini shaker with ice, a shot (1½ ounces) of rum, whiskey, or vodka and 1 cup of peach cobbler. Shake and serve over ice in a rocks glass.

FLOWER-POWER ICED TEA

This drink was an all-time favorite at my house back in the day. I took the classic recipe of vanilla-and-flower-infused black tea and flipped it by making it with green tea. You can abuse this drink with a healthy dose of rum or whiskey.

MAKES **1 gallon**   PREP TIME **20 minutes**

14 cups water
1 ¼ cups superfine or raw sugar
1   vanilla bean
10 tsps. loose Earl Grey green tea
     or 10 tea bags

1   tbsp. fresh or dried lavender heads
2   cups ice cubes
     Sweetened condensed milk or
     coconut milk, for garnish (optional)
     Rum or whiskey, to taste (optional)

1. In a 6-quart pot set on high, bring the water to a boil.
2. Place the sugar in a small bowl.
3. With a paring knife, slice the vanilla bean lengthwise and open it to expose the seeds. With the back of the knife, scrap the seeds onto the sugar. Mix well and pour the sugar into a small sauce pan.
4. Add two cups of the boiling water to the sugar, stirring to combine. Set aside for 20 minutes to cool.
5. Add the tea and lavender heads to the remaining boiling water, turn off the heat, and let steep for 15 to 20 minutes.
6. Strain tea through a fine-mesh sieve or cheesecloth.
7. Add the ice cubes to a pitcher or jug, then pour in the tea and vanilla syrup. Serve over ice and top with a tablespoon of sweetened condensed milk, if you like. For a cocktail, fill a shaker with ice, a shot (1½ ounces) of rum or whiskey, and 1 cup of tea. Shake well and serve over ice in a rocks glass.

CUCUMBER MINT-ADE

MAKES **about 1 quart**   PREP TIME **30 minutes plus 2 hours for chilling**

6 cups water
1 cup superfine or raw sugar,
   plus more for rimming glasses
6 to 8 sprigs of mint, plus more
   for garnish

4 English cucumbers, peeled or
   unpeeled, chopped into 1-inch-
   thick slices (reserve half a
   cucumber to cut into slices
   for garnish)

1 17-oz. container of coconut water,
   preferably Vita Coco (with or
   without pulp)
   Vodka, preferably Ketel One,
   to taste (optional)

1. In a small sauce pan set on high, combine 1 cup of the water, the sugar, and mint. Bring to a boil. Reduce heat to low and simmer for 15 minutes. Strain the syrup into a small bowl; discard the mint. Set syrup aside to cool.
2. In a blender, purée the cucumber and remaining water.
3. Using a fine mesh strainer, strain the mixture over a large bowl, pushing down with the back of a spoon to squeeze through as much liquid as possible.
4. Add the coconut water and mint syrup, stirring to combine. Cover and refrigerate for 2 hours before serving.
5. To serve, pour the liquid into a pitcher; coat the rim of a glass with sugar, add ice, pour in the mint-ade, and top with a mint sprig and cucumber slice. For a cocktail, just stir in with a shot (1½ ounces) of vodka.

DANTE FRIED CHICKEN
BOOTLEG SCREENING PARTY
APRIL 22ND SUNDAY 6–10PM
COCONUT FRIED CHICKEN/TOFU
COLLARD GREEN YAM EGG ROLLS
OPEN VODKA BAR 6–9
49 Ann Street 3rd floor
$10 (receive a KFC RIP vip card)

I'm passionate about the rubs, spice mixes, and flours in this chapter: I never cook without them. The best thing to do is make them in big batches and use them as necessary. As for the sauces, we take them hella serious in my family; no, we don't play. In my house growing up, every meal was complemented by at least four or five sauces. Sauces are a cook's best friend—if your dish becomes compromised, a good sauce will save your ass in a minute.

Finally, you're gonna love the recipes for making your own tempeh and seitan in this chapter. Once you take a bite of the real thing, the store-bought stuff will never taste the same.

SPICE MIXES&RUBS

Here are a few essential DFC home base spices you can easily create at your crib—they'll add flare to everything and anything you cook up. Before you start, I strongly urge you to invest in an electric spice grinder and mortar and pestle if you don't already have these tools in your kit.

DFC FISH FRY SPICE MIX

In addition to using this mix for your fish fries, try it as a shrimp or crab boil, or add a ½ teaspoon to 1 teaspoon or more to taste to ceviche.

MAKES **about 4 cups**

¼ cup cinnamon
¼ cup allspice
½ cup freshly grated nutmeg
2 tbsps. mace
½ cumin seeds or powder
½ cup celery seed

10 dried bay leaves or 2 tbsps. bay leaf powder
½ cup mustard seeds
½ cup pink Brazilian peppercorns
½ cup black peppercorns or ¼ cup freshly ground black pepper

¼ cup red pepper flakes
¼ cup whole cloves or 2 tbsps. ground cloves
4 tbsps. poppy seeds
2 tbsps. fennel seeds (optional)
3 to 4 tbsps. sea salt (optional; see Note)

SALT TO TASTE

I like to add the salt directly to the recipe and omit it from the spice mix. This gives you more control (if you are on a low-sodium diet, for instance) and the flexibility to use it with a wide variety of dishes.

1. In a medium bowl, combine the cinnamon, allspice, nutmeg, and mace. If you are using the bay leaf powder, ground black pepper, and ground cloves, add those, too.
2. In a spice grinder, grind the cumin seeds, celery seed, bay leaves (if using), mustard seeds, pink and black peppercorns (if using), red pepper flakes, whole cloves (if using), poppy seeds, and fennel seeds (if using).
3. Add the freshly ground spices to the cinnamon mixture, stirring to combine. Add salt to taste. Store in an airtight container for up to 6 months.

ALL-PURPOSE CHICKEN SPICE

This mix is great for baked chicken or any poultry dish. Add it to gravies and stuffings as well as mashed potatoes.

MAKES **about 1½ cups**

20 whole cloves, freshly ground, or 1 tbsp. ground cloves
6 tbsps. dried parsley, crushed fine
2 tbsps. dried sage leaves, crushed fine
2 tbsps. dried thyme leaves, crushed fine

1 tbsp. dried marjoram, crushed fine
2 tbsps. herbes de Provence, crushed fine

2 tbsps. granulated onion
2 tbsps. granulated garlic
2½ tsps. sea salt

1. If using whole cloves, grind them in a spice grinder or with a mortar and pestle.
2. In a small bowl, combine the ground cloves with the remaining spices. Store in an airtight container for up to 6 months.

VAR·I·A·TION
BBQ CHICKEN SPICE MIX

Use this as a dry coating for any white fish, shrimp, or clams.

1 recipe All-Purpose Chicken Spice
3 tbsps. light brown sugar
1 tsp. ground mustard

In a medium bowl, combine all ingredients thoroughly. Store in an airtight container for up to 6 months.

FRIED CHICKEN SPICE MIX

MAKES **about 4 cups; 5 cups with additional spices added**

1 cup sweet paprika
1 cup granulated garlic
1 cup granulated onion
¼ cup freshly ground black pepper
¼ cup sea salt

For additional kick, add:
¼ cup celery seed
¼ cup cayenne pepper
¼ cup white pepper

1½ tbsps. dried sage, crushed fine
1½ tbsps. dried oregano, crushed fine
1½ tbsps. mustard seeds, crushed fine

In a medium bowl, combine all ingredients thoroughly. Store in airtight container for up to 6 months.

MEAT RUB

This rub is great on steaks, pot roast, lamb, goat, burgers, and *carne asada* (Mexican roasted beef). Sprinkle your steaks with 1 or 2 teaspoons of this mix, rub it in, place in an airtight container or Ziploc bag, and refrigerate overnight.

MAKES **about 2 cups**

¾ cup sweet paprika
1 tbsp. cumin seeds or powder
3 tbsps. freshly ground
   black pepper

3 tbsps. chili powder
3 tbsps. granulated garlic
3 tbsps. granulated onion
4 tsps. cayenne pepper

4 tsps. dried chipotle peppers,
   stemmed and seeded, or powder
3 tsps. freshly grated nutmeg
1 tbsp. dried mixed Italian herbs or
   herbes de Provence, crushed fine

1. If using cumin seeds and dried chipotle peppers, grind them in a spice grinder or with a mortar and pestle.
2. In a medium bowl, combine all ingredients thoroughly. Store in an airtight container for up to 6 months.

DFC BBQ MEAT RUB

This rub will create a nice crust, or "bark," on your red meat when smoked or grilled.

1 recipe DFC Meat Rub
⅓ cup light brown sugar, packed
4 tbsps. best-quality cocoa powder
   (Cacao Barry Cocoa Powder,
   for instance)

In a medium bowl, combine all ingredients thoroughly. Store in an airtight container for up to 6 months.

FLOUR MIXES

When time is tight, it's a godsend to have batches of DFC spiced flours and baking flours at the ready. Mix up a batch and dry-keep them in the cupboard—they'll last there for up to 6 months. FYI, you don't have to use these flours just for deep frying chicken, tofu, or fish; get involved with zucchini, mozzarella, calamari, onions, string beans, or anything else you can think of. You can also use this to sear off your pot roast or to thicken and flavor next-level gravies.

FISH FRY SPICED FLOUR

Use this as a dry coating for any white fish, shrimp, or clams.

MAKES **about 8 cups**

2 cups DFC Fish Fry Mix
12 cups coarse yellow cornmeal
5 cups all-purpose flour

In a large bowl, combine all ingredients thoroughly. Store in an airtight container for up to 6 months.

FRIED-CHICKEN SPICED FLOUR

MAKES **about 19 cups**

1 recipe Fried Chicken Spice Mix
10 cups all-purpose flour
3 cups white cornmeal
¾ cup baking soda, cornstarch, or potato starch

In an extra large bowl, combine all ingredients thoroughly. Store in an airtight container for up to 6 months.

SELF-RISING FLOUR

Make your own self-rising flour to use in crispy batters, thick gravy and stews, pancakes, biscuits, and waffles.

MAKES **6 cups**

6 cups all-purpose flour
1 tbsp. sea salt
3 tbsps. baking powder

In a large bowl, combine all ingredients thoroughly. Store in an airtight container for up to 6 months.

THE BITS*

MAKES **about 4 lbs.**

1 16 oz. container of steel-cut oats (not instant)
6 English muffins, split
1 12-oz. box of Corn Flakes
½ 12-oz. box of plain shredded wheat

2 cups sliced almonds (raw or toasted)
2 cups sesame seeds
½ cup poppy seeds

CRUNCHY BITS

You can add just about anything crunchy to the bits mix: stale crackers, nuts, flax seeds, potato chips, tortilla chips, pita, and any variety of bread. Grind them up and toss them in. You can even add corn bread and biscuits so long as you dry them out in an oven first.

1. Preheat oven to 350°F.
2. Cut the English muffins into bite-size pieces and place them in a single layer on a baking sheet. Bake for 10 minutes.
3. In a food processor, grind the muffin pieces until fine crumbs form.
4. In a large bowl, hand-crush the corn flakes and shredded wheat to a medium-fine crumble. Add the almonds, sesame seeds, and poppy seeds.
5. Pour in the muffin crumbs and combine thoroughly. Store the bits in an airtight container for up to 3 months.

VARIATION! SAVORY BITS

Season the bits with fresh or dried herbs, salt, and pepper and toast them in a 350°F oven for 5 minutes. Use the toasted bits in salads and as a topping for your macaroni and cheese or any casserole. Savory Bits will keep in airtight container for up to 3 months.

VARIATION SWEET BITS

Next time a baking recipe calls for cookie crust, just use this instead.

To the basic bits mixture, add stale cookies, scones, biscuits, and candied nuts and/or seeds. Grind them in a food processor until fine crumbs form. Sweet Bits will keep in airtight container for up to 2 months.

STOCKS

The base for my stocks is for the most part the same, with different proteins added as the dominant flavor. I don't skim the fat off my stocks as they cook, but you can. I find that it's easier to remove the fat once the stock has cooled and the fat has congealed. Stock is always better after it sits overnight and the flavors have melded together, but feel free to use the stock right away. Stocks can be stored in airtight containers in the refrigerator for up to 5 days or in the freezer for up to 6 months.

I recently started using coconut water in place of water for stocks. I recommend doing a mixture of water and coconut water at first to ease yourself into the 100% coconut water approach. If are a coconut fanatic, like me, you'll love it. Keep in mind that some brands of coconut water have pulp, and you may want to strain it before adding it to your stock pot.

VEGGIE STOCK

Homemade veggie stock is so much better than the store-bought stuff. Never go without homemade in your fridge or freezer, if you can.

MAKES **about 10 cups**

A WORD ON BOUILLON PASTE

You can skip making your own stock and make a broth using high-quality bouillon concentrate instead. I use it all the time to flavor many of my dishes. Superior Touch's "Better Than Bouillon" paste blows the door off the hinges of most brands I've tried and comes in a rainbow of flavors, from mushroom to lobster. As good as it is, though, I will not use store-bought bouillon to make dishes like gumbo or homemade chicken soup. There are no shortcuts when making these! Remember to follow the instructions on the label.

10 to 15 cups water or coconut water
2 dried bay leaves
4 garlic cloves, skin on and smashed
4 carrots, coarsely chopped
1 large white or yellow onion, skin on and quartered
4 whole scallions, rubbed (that is, crushed like you would a garlic clove)

5 celery stalks, coarsely chopped
 All leaves from 1 bunch of celery
1 bunch fresh parsley, rubbed
1 or 2 rutabaga or turnips, coarsely chopped (optional)
1 tsp. salt or 1 tbsp. amino acids, preferably Bragg's
 Freshly ground black pepper

1. Put all ingredients in a large stock pot, and fill it with enough water to cover the vegetables by a few inches. Season with salt or aminos, if using, and pepper, and set the heat on high.
2. Bring to a boil, then reduce heat to low and simmer for 1 to 5 hours. The longer you simmer, the more intense the flavor.
3. Discard all the veggies and strain the stock through a fine-mesh sieve or cheesecloth fitted to a strainer.

CHICKEN STOCK

MAKES **about 10 cups**

Veggie Stock ingredients
(see opposite page)
4 lbs. chicken parts
(any combination)

1. To the Veggie Stock ingredients, add the chicken parts. Fill the stock pot with enough water to cover the veggies and chicken by an inch.
2. Bring to a boil, then reduce heat to low and simmer for 1 to 5 hours. The longer you simmer, the more intense the flavor.
3. Discard all the veggies, but reserve the chicken parts. Place the chicken parts in a separate bowl to cool.
4. Strain the stock through a fine-mesh sieve or cheesecloth fitted to a strainer.
5. When cool, pick the chicken from the bones, discarding the bones, skin, and cartilage. The chicken can be used for enchiladas, tamales, salads, or any recipe where you add flavor back in.

←GUMBO·STOCK→

MAKES **about 10 cups**

Veggie Stock ingredients
(see opposite page)
1 5-lb. chicken, cut into 8 pieces
1 smoked ham hock
2 whole fish carcasses, such as salmon, catfish, or red snapper
1 cup dried shrimp

1. To the Veggie Stock ingredients, add the chicken, ham hock, fish parts, and dried shrimp. Fill the stock pot with enough water to cover everything by an inch.
2. Bring to a boil, then reduce heat to low and simmer for 1 to 5 hours. The longer you simmer, the more intense the flavor.
3. Discard all the veggies, fish pieces, ham hock, and dried shrimp, but reserve the chicken parts. Place the chicken parts in a separate bowl to cool.
4. Strain the stock through a fine-mesh sieve or cheesecloth fitted to a strainer.
5. When cool, pick the chicken from the bones, discarding the bones, skin, and cartilage. The chicken can be used for enchiladas, tamales, salads, or any recipe where you add flavor back in.

BEEF STOCK

Got beef? Here is a basic stock recipe that can be used fresh or frozen.

MAKES **10 cups**

- 3 lbs. beef or veal bones
- 2 lbs. stew beef or beef scraps (not fat)
- 1 large white or yellow onion, skin on and quartered
- 4 garlic cloves, skin on and smashed
- 4 carrots, coarsely chopped
- 1 or 2 rutabaga or turnips, coarsely chopped (optional)
- 1 tbsp. olive oil
  Sea salt and freshly ground pepper
- 2 cups red wine

- 10 to 15 cups water or coconut water
- 2 dried bay leaves
- 4 whole scallions, rubbed (that is, crushed like you would a garlic clove)

- 5 celery stalks, coarsely chopped
  All leaves from 1 bunch of celery
- 1 bunch fresh parsley, rubbed
- 1 tsp. salt or 1 tbsp. amino acids, preferably Bragg's

1. Preheat oven to 375°F.
2. In a 6-quart Dutch oven, combine the bones, stew meat, and the onion, garlic, carrots, and rutabaga or turnips, if using.
3. Add the olive oil and salt and pepper to taste, and toss to coat. Bake, covered, until browned, 45 to 60 minutes.
4. Transfer the veggies, bones, and stew meat to a medium bowl. Set aside.
5. Set the Dutch oven on medium heat and deglaze with the red wine, using a wooden spoon to break up all the bits stuck to the bottom of the pot.
6. Return the veggies, bones, and stew meat to the Dutch oven and add the remaining ingredients.
7. Fill the Dutch oven with enough water to cover everything by an inch.
8. Bring to a boil, then reduce heat to low and simmer for 1 to 5 hours. The longer you simmer, the more intense the flavor.
9. Discard all the veggies and bones, but reserve the stew meat, which can be used for enchiladas, tamales, salads, or any recipe where you add flavor back in.
10. Strain the stock through a fine-mesh sieve or cheesecloth fitted to a strainer.

SEITAN STOCK

MAKES **10 cups**

Veggie Stock ingredients
(page 194)
4 thumb-size pieces of fresh ginger, skin on and quartered
1 cup amino acids or soy sauce
2 jalapeños, sliced in half and seeded
1 tbsp. toasted sesame oil
1 tsp. miso paste

1. In a large stock pot, add all of the ingredients to the Veggie Stock ingredients and fill it with enough water to cover the vegetables by a few inches. Set the heat on high.
2. Bring to a boil, then reduce heat to low and simmer for 1 to 5 hours. The longer you simmer, the more intense the flavor.
3. Discard all the veggies and strain the stock through a fine-mesh sieve or cheesecloth fitted to a strainer.

 PROTEINS

TEMPEH

The Indonesian technique of fermenting soybeans and binding them together with an edible mold creates tempeh, a protein with nutty flavor and a distinct texture that's something truly special for the veg heads. I use garbanzo beans. Either way, tempeh crumbles really well and holds up just like ground beef in sauces—you can make the most amazing sloppy joe with it.

MAKES 1½ lbs.   **PREP TIME 30 to 45 minutes, plus 48 hours for soaking and fermenting**

3 cups dry garbanzo beans
6 tsps. veggie bouillon paste, preferably Superior Touch

2½ tbsps. apple cider vinegar, preferably Bragg's
1½ tsps. tempeh starter (see Note)

TEMPEH STARTER

Tempeh starter culture kits are extremely hard to find in the States. Purchase one online. Beware that some companies are rip-offs (yes, I got gaffled). I've tried a company called Top Culture, and they are legit.

MAKING TEMPEH NOTE

Make your homemade tempeh in the morning so that the heat of the day will get the spore culture activated. After it has established, it will continue at slightly lower temps.

1. Place the garbanzos in a large bowl and fill with water until the beans are covered by 3 inches. Let the beans soak overnight.
2. The next day, drain the beans. In a 4-quart pot on medium-high, add beans, bouillon, and enough water to cover the beans. Cook the beans, uncovered, until soft but still firm (slightly underdone), about 30 minutes. Drain the beans and let cool for 10 minutes.
3. Transfer the beans to a food processor and pulse a few times to form a coarse paste, with some whole beans remaining. Transfer to a large bowl and add the vinegar. Mix to combine.
4. Add the tempeh starter and mix thoroughly. Spread the mixture into a baking dish or pan. Pack it down tight, and cover the dish or pan with aluminum foil.
5. Pierce foil with a fork several times, and cover dish or pan with a clean dish or kitchen towel. Place in a warm spot, 85°F to 90°F, for 24 hours. Or place the foil-covered and vented dish in the oven on the lowest temp. Prop oven door open with a jar lid (see Note).
6. After 24 to 30 hours, the tempeh will be ready. The finished tempeh should smell pleasant, with a rich mushroom-like fragrance. Patches of gray or black coloration indicates that your tempeh has cultured correctly. If it smells off-putting or has green mold or a slimy texture, discard and try again. Don't sweat the fuzzy culture growing on the top of it—this is normal and means it has fermented properly.
7. Cut the tempeh into squares and wrap the slices individually in wax paper or stack, with the top side facing down, in an airtight container and store in the refrigerator for up to 5 days or in the freezer for up to 2 months.

TEMPEH & SEITAN

There's been a lot of confusion about tempeh and seitan, so let's set the record straight here. Tempeh is different from tofu and other veggie proteins; it's made from fermented soy beans and has an entirely unique texture. Contrary to what some believe, seitan is not tofu. A popular source of veggie protein, seitan is actually wheat gluten. It's made by extracting the proteins from flour, kneading them into a dense dough, and then simmering pieces of it like dumplings.

SEITAN

Seitan is an awesome protein that's all veggie, all the time: it's made from the earth. A lot of people say its texture reminds them of steak, but I beg to differ. It has its own thang poppin', so let's just enjoy it for what it is: kneaded wheat gluten simmered in a flavorful broth. You can use seitan for pretty much any recipe that would require red meat; for instance, it makes a banging faux beef and broccoli stir-fry.

MAKES **1½ lbs.** PREP AND COOKING TIME **1 hour 45 minutes**

- 2 cups gluten flour
- 2 tsps. garlic powder
- 2 tsps. ground ginger
- 1 tsp. crushed chili flakes
- 2 tsps. veggie bouillon paste, preferably Superior Touch

- 1¼ cups hot water
- 3 tbsps. light tamari, Bragg's liquid amino acids, or soy sauce

- 1 to 3 tsps. toasted sesame oil (optional)
- 1 recipe Seitan Stock (page 197, warmed in a large stock pot on low)

1. In a large bowl, add the garlic powder and ginger to flour and stir until thoroughly combined.
2. Mix liquids together and add to flour mixture all at once. Mix vigorously with a fork. When it forms a stiff elastic dough, knead it 10 to 15 times.
3. Let the dough rest for 5 minutes, then knead it a few more times. Let it rest another 15 minutes.
4. Cut gluten into 6 to 8 pieces and stretch each into a thin cutlet.
5. Add seitan to the warm stock (Seitan will expand to 3 times its original size, so use a large stock pot.) Increase the heat to high and bring to a boil. Reduce the heat to low and simmer seitan for 1 hour.
6. Remove the seitan from the broth and let cool to room temperature. You can refrigerate it for up to 5 days or it will keep in an airtight Ziploc bag or container in the freezer for up to 1 month.

sSSAUCES!

BOUJEE RANCH SAUCE

For those of you unfamiliar with the term "boujee," it means high-class or gentrified (from the French for "bourgeois"). That's right, we're taking ranch sauce uptown. Made from dried ingredients, including dehydrated shallots, carrots, chives, parsley, celery, and peppers, I guess it's kind of like the OG Hidden Valley Ranch dressing of the 1950s—they didn't use chemicals back then, and there ain't a lick of chemicals in mine. It's ideal for dipping finger foods, such as wings and fried seafood—yum. This recipe is an homage to my friend Teresa, aka TT, who came up with the name for it. TT's always mocked my food for its eccentricity, and I suppose this sauce is no different.

MAKES **about 1 ½ cups**   PREP AND COOKING TIME **45 minutes**

2 tsps. dehydrated carrots
1 tsp. dehydrated shallots
1 tsp. sweet pepper flakes
1 cup buttermilk
½ cup mayonnaise
1 tsp. fresh lemon juice
⅛ tsp. celery seed

⅛ tsp. paprika
¼ tsp. ground mustard
⅛ tsp. paprika
¼ tsp. ground mustard
1 tbsp. chopped fresh parsley
1 tsp. chopped fresh chives

¼ tsp. dried dill (or 1 tsp. chopped
     fresh dill)
½ tsp. sea salt
   Freshly ground black pepper
4 tbsps. grated Parmesan (optional)
   A pinch of white sugar (optional)

1. In a small bowl, combine the dehydrated carrots, dehydrated shallots, and pepper flakes. Add enough water to cover them, and set aside to soak for 30 minutes.
2. Meanwhile, in a medium bowl, stir together the buttermilk and mayonnaise until thoroughly combined. Add the lemon juice, celery seed, paprika, ground mustard, parsley, chives, dill, salt, pepper, and Parmesan and sugar, if using. Stir well, taste it, and adjust the seasoning with more salt and pepper, if necessary. The sauce can be refrigerated in an airtight container for up to a week. Yep, we flossy!

COCONANA CURRY KETCHUP

I had plenty of banana ketchup growing up, introduced to me by my Filipino best friend. But it wasn't until I went to Berlin, where I found their curry ketchup—influenced by British and Indian cultures—that I realized ketchup's potential. The Germans slather their version all over their national hot dog, the currywurst. I was inspired to take curry ketchup back to the Philippines, so to speak, and then got mad scientist with it, tossing in everything from raisins to cloves to whiskey—and, of course, bananas. Use this like you'd use your regular ketchup, on all the usuals: burgers, dogs, fried chicken, steak, and any type of fries.

MAKES **3 to 4 cups**   PREP AND COOKING TIME **2 hours**

½ cup golden raisins
½ cup plus 2 tbsps. whiskey
4 large, very ripe bananas, peeled and sliced
⅓ cup chopped sweet onion
2 garlic cloves, chopped
2 chipotle peppers *en adobo*, minced, plus 2 tbsps. adobo sauce

1 jalapeño, ribs and seeds removed, chopped
½ cup dark brown sugar, packed
1½ tsps. sea salt
1 cup tomato paste
¼ cup agave nectar
3 to 4 cups Veggie Stock (page 194)
1 dried bay leaf

1 cup apple cider vinegar, preferably Bragg's
2 tsps. allspice
1 tsp. cinnamon
½ tsp. freshly grated nutmeg
¼ tsp. ground cloves
2 tbsps. curry powder

1. In a small bowl, add the raisins and 2 tablespoons of the whiskey. Let soak for 10 minutes.
2. In a food processor, combine the raisin-whiskey mixture, bananas, onion, garlic, chipotle peppers, adobo sauce, jalapeño, brown sugar, salt, tomato paste, agave nectar, the remaining whiskey, and 3 cups of the veggie stock. Process until smooth. Add the mixture to a 4-quart sauce pan set on medium. Add the bay leaf and cider vinegar.
3. Meanwhile, in a 7-inch pan set on medium-high, combine the allspice, cinnamon, nutmeg, cloves, curry powder. Toast until fragrant, about 2 minutes.
4. Stir the spices into the banana mixture, increase the heat to medium-high and bring it to a boil, stirring often. Reduce heat to low and simmer for 1 hour, whisking occasionally. If the ketchup becomes too thick, add some of the remaining stock.
5. The ketchup is ready when it coats the back of a metal spoon. Remove the bay leaf and let the ketchup cool for 10 minutes before transferring it to sterilized jars or airtight containers. The ketchup will keep in the refrigerator for up to 1 month.

APRICOT CRACK SAUCE

This sauce has been with me from the start—I've been making it for 13 years for my parties, events, and catering. It's a real game-changer; trust me when I say you need it in your life. I think of it as Credit Crunch Fried Chicken's partner—they taste great together, and both have been with me forever. Made with various hot peppers, a dab of apple cider, ginger, and dried apricots, the sauce has fans from New York to Nigeria, where one of my friend's moms was knocked out by it. She put it on everything, although she thinks that it goes best with seafood. I hope it reaches the international stardom of Sriracha, one of my personal favorites.

MAKES **about 4 cups**   PREP AND COOKING TIME **2 hours**

3½ cups water
1 lb. dried apricots, whole
11 cups superfine or raw sugar
2 tbsps. minced fresh ginger
4 dried aji panca chilies, stems and seeds removed

2 tsps. canola oil
10 Tabasco or serrano chilies, stems, ribs, and seeds removed, diced
12 red jalapeños, ribs and seeds removed, diced
10 Scotch bonnet peppers, stems, ribs, and seeds removed, diced

1½ tbsps. minced garlic
¾ cup thinly sliced onion
¾ tsps. sea salt
½ cup honey
1 cup apple cider vinegar, preferably Bragg's

SAFETY NOTE

Open the windows in your kitchen when sautéing the hot peppers. This is an intense process; wear a medical mask if you wish, and if you have an exhaust fan, blast it. Oh yeah, DON'T breathe directly over the peppers. It will attack you like pepper spray! Alternatively, sauté the peppers outdoors on your BBQ grill by either using the fancy-pants burner or by setting the pan directly on the grill grate.

1. In a 6-quart pot set on high, combine 1 ½ cups of the water, the apricots, sugar, ginger, and aji panca chilies and bring to a boil. Reduce the heat to low and simmer for 30 minutes. Remove from heat and cool the mixture to room temperature.

2. In a blender, purée the cooled mixture and set aside. Wash the pot; you'll use it again.

3. In the 6-quart pot set on medium-high, heat the oil until it shimmers. Add the Tabasco or serranos, jalapeños, Scotch bonnets, garlic, onion, and salt and sauté for 3 minutes (see Note).

4. Add the remaining 2 cups water and continue to cook, stirring occasionally, until peppers are very soft and almost all of the liquid has evaporated, about 20 minutes. Remove from heat and let the peppers cool to room temperature.

5. In a blender, purée the cooled peppers and the honey while slowly adding the vinegar. Add water if the consistency is too thick.

6. Pour the pepper purée back into the pot. Add the apricot purée, stirring to combine. Simmer the sauce on low heat for 30 minutes, skimming any foam that may form on the surface.

7. Taste and season with more salt, if necessary. Transfer the sauce to sterilized pint jars or bottles and secure with airtight lids. The sauce can be stored in the refrigerator for up to 3 months.

BLUEBERRY-GUINNESS BBQ SAUCE

This smoky, layered, full-bodied BBQ sauce is versatile as hell. I use it for our DFC Guinness BBQ Brisket, but it's actually one of the DFC mother sauces. The mix of sweet and spicy in this one gives it the perfect kick, making it an insane complement to all sorts of dishes. Use it as a dip for chips and crudités, spoon it over sautéed veggies, or serve it as a sauce for just about any protein you like. I've even made ice cream with it . . . hell, yes, I did!

MAKES 6 cups   **PREP AND COOKING TIME 45 minutes, plus 1 to 2 hours for simmering**

2 tbsps. chili powder
1 tbsp. ground cumin
1 tbsp. herbes de Provence
1 tsp. ground cloves
1 tsp. freshly grated nutmeg
1 tsp. allspice
1 tbsp. cinnamon
1 tsp. sea salt
    Freshly ground black pepper
3 tbsps. canola oil

1 small onion, chopped
1 serrano chili, ribs and seeds removed, minced
2 celery stalks, chopped
2 garlic cloves, minced
1 cup Guinness stout
1 shot of espresso
2 cups ketchup
½ cup yellow mustard
1 cup molasses

1 cup dark brown sugar, packed
1 to 4 tsps. Sriracha, depending on how hot you like your sauce
½ of a 3 ½-oz. good-quality dark chocolate (Ghirardelli, for example)
1½ cups dried blueberries
1 dried bay leaf

1. In a small bowl, combine the chili powder, cumin, herbes de Provence, cloves, nutmeg, allspice, cinnamon, salt, and pepper to taste.
2. In a 4-quart sauce pan set on medium-high, heat the oil until it shimmers. Add the onion, serrano chili, and celery and sauté until soft and translucent, about 5 minutes. Add the garlic and sauté for 1 minute more. Pour in the dry spices and stir to combine. Cook for 2 minutes.
3. Add the Guinness and espresso, stir, and reduce heat to low. Simmer for 15 minutes. Remove the sauce from the heat and let cool slightly.
4. Transfer the sauce to a blender and purée until smooth. Pour it back into the sauce pan, set it on medium, and add the ketchup, mustard, molasses, brown sugar, and Sriracha to taste.
5. Stir in the chocolate, dried blueberries, and bay leaf, and reduce the heat to low. Simmer for an hour or two, stirring occasionally. The consistency should be slightly thick and very velvety, almost like a chocolate or mole sauce. Remove the bay leaf before using the sauce. The sauce will keep in a sterilized jar or airtight container in the refrigerator for up to 2 months.

HOTTY TOTTY SPICY MUSTARD

My cousin Promise Smith goes crazy over this mustard. We both have a taste for strangely strong, spicy mustards, and after feeling unsatisfied with the majority of mild-ass varieties we perfected a wasabi- and whiskey-based banger, licked with honey to round down the intensity. Phenomenal with fried chicken, fries, and corn dogs, it's also great on sandwiches, crackers, or salami. I've even had it with grilled veggies and blackened tempeh. You get the picture—for fans of spicy food, it's perfect with just about anything.

MAKES **about 4 cups**   PREP AND COOKING TIME **30 minutes, plus 2 hours refrigeration**

1½ cups plus up to 4 tbsps. boiling water
A pinch of sea salt
1½ cups honey
2 tbsps. prepared horseradish
½ cup apple cider vinegar, preferably Bragg's
¼ tsp. cayenne pepper

¼ to 1 tsp. Sriracha
2 cups light mustard seeds
2 tbsps. ground mustard
½ tsp. turmeric
3 tsps. garlic powder
A pinch of freshly ground black pepper
2 tbsps. whole-wheat flour

1. In medium glass bowl, combine 1½ cups of the boiling water, salt, honey, horseradish, cider vinegar, cayenne pepper, and Sriracha. Set aside.
2. In mortar, spice grinder, or clean coffee grinder, combine the mustard seeds, ground mustard, turmeric, garlic powder, black pepper, and whole-wheat flour, and pulverize until finely ground. I like my mustard smooth, but you can leave it rougher if you prefer a grainy texture.
3. Add mustard powder mixture to honey mixture, and stir until smooth. Add more boiling water slowly by the tablespoon until it's the consistency of runny, French's mustard. It will thicken as it stands.
4. Scrape down the sides of the bowl and cover it with plastic wrap. Refrigerate the mustard for 2 hours before serving. If mustard thickens too much, add more boiling water, a tablespoon at a time. Transfer the mustard to sterilized jars or airtight containers. The mustard will keep for up to 2 months in the refrigerator.

DFC CREW, NaNa, MeMe, Jason Thome, David Sarussi, Gary Hunt, Christine Kajetzke, Kat O'Reilly, TT, Jean, Rogerio Cubas & Family, Bing Gonzales, David Belisle, Liv L'Raynge, Chase Bingham, MJ Zilla, Ms. Rawls, Marcus Price, Purple Crush, my Swedish Family, Tomas Botex, Rusty Madison Myer, Nancy Douglas, Steven Douglas, Tamera Holding, Katherine Bates (not the actress), Converse, Earnest Endeavors, LuckyMe, All the ChickenHeadz (You Know Who You Are), Teh family, Freddie Janssen, Shaniqwa Jarvis, Pixie Felton, Ciaran McNeaney, Tom McCarthy, Alex Stevenson, Amber Bessey, Franky Lisk, Will Rowe, all the artists Dante has had the pleasure of cooking with, and all the fam involved in our first London, NY, LA shows and beyond!! There would be no this without you.

Love from the Design Team
Without the following people, this book would not have been possible: Johnny Por Taing, Daniel Choe, Albert Ignacio, Matthew Goodrich, Josh Shaub, David Belisle, John Toga Cox, Whitney Young, Nathaniel Matthews, Kevin Harris, James Hughes, Omar Almufti, Alex Merto, King Texas, TONE, Joseph Bradley, Owen Hoskins, Allison Meierding, Nathan Cowen, Zakee, Joel Roman, Greg Lapidus, Michael Rosenblatt, Dan Petruzzi, Dave Riley, Colton Corry, Michael Simons.